TWICE ROUND THE BLACK CHURCH

Twice Round the Black Church

EARLY MEMORIES
OF IRELAND
AND ENGLAND

Austin Clarke

MOYTURA PRESS
DUBLIN

First published 1962 by
Routledge & Kegan Paul Ltd,
London.

This edition published by
Moytura Press, 3 The Dale,
Stillorgan, Co. Dublin.

ISBN 1-871305-02-0

This edition was printed by
Colour Books Ltd., Dublin

Contents

Acknowledgements

Some of the episodes included in this book have already appeared in a small, semi-private publication, *First Visit to England.*
The translation on page 3 is taken from *Figures of Speech or Figures of Thought*, 2nd Series, by Ananda K. Coomaraswamy (Luzac and Co.).

To my niece, Aileen Dempsey

One

I

FOR many years I could never hear without a momentary feeling of uneasiness, the name of Shakespeare mentioned by anyone. The very syllables had a sinister ring for me because of the dread that name caused me in childhood. There was an empty room at the top of our house and on the wall, between the fireplace and the window, almost hidden in the gloom, hung a small portrait in oils. Dim and yellowed by time, that picture showed the head of a man of strange appearance, for he had long hair and below his pointed beard was some kind of wide collar brim. His face was melancholy and yet it always seemed to me that there was a sneer upon those bearded lips. I cannot remember when the portrait first stirred my curiosity, but one day I asked the name of the man and I was told in jest or ignorance, that it was Shakespeare. The very name was foreign and had an inimical sound – who could be this moody stranger shaking a spear when he was angry? Children rarely look up when they are playing with toys on the floor, for they are too busy with their own imaginings, but one day, when I had strayed into that vacant room and was amusing myself, I happened to glance towards the portrait and saw, to my astonishment, that the eyes of the man were watching me. I turned away, then looked up, and once more his eyes met mine. I got to my feet and, as I did so, those eyes turned to watch every movement I made. I backed towards the door and that look still followed me, half mournful, half accusing. I did not tell anyone what had happened but I did not venture into the room again for more than a few seconds at a time except when I was with grown-ups. Emboldened by their company, I learned to play a fearful but exciting game. I moved slowly here and there about the room, knowing that wherever I went, those eyes followed me. I pretended not to look, I talked to my elders, then swung around sharply. I was still being watched. The searching gaze was always the same, so melancholy and accusing that I began to feel a sense of guilt, began to wonder what evil I could have committed. Guilt and fear mingled in my mind and I was certain, because of his name, that the stranger was treacherous, that his anger could be terrible when it was aroused. Sometimes, greatly daring, I crept up the stairs and opened the door very quietly, very quickly, and peeped in. Every time I did so, his eyes were looking straight at me.

But soon that daylight game of hide-and-seek had dire consequences. At night, before I went to sleep, I could not help thinking of the portrait in the empty room upstairs, for I was certain by now that it was alive. The faint glow of the altar light in the colza bowl was powerless to protect me from the mystery of the canvas. Stories of witches, ogres and magicians were fearful enough, but they were remote and, when I thought of the picture books from which, they emerged, my anxiety could be dispelled. But this danger was different, for there were only two short flights of stairs between it and me. Children can enact in their little way the primary myths, find for themselves the ancient ritual of fear. So, night after night, my mind was drawn in obedient horror towards that room upstairs. It had become the forbidden chamber of legend, dreadful in darkness, and I was as powerless to resist it as Bluebeard's youngest wife when she turned the key in the lock. Were it not for the childish alarms which all of us remember so well, we would forget the power of our earliest imaginings, forget those first years when the mind seemed to part so readily from the body. Night after night I thought that I was actually climbing those two flights of stairs, compelled by the presence of that man in the frame. But the moment I got to the door of the forbidden room, the real struggle began. It is easy to forget not only the workings of our early imagination, but also the power of the will when we first discover its use, that determination shown by children when they are crossed or in the sulks. The struggle between my will and imagination was a mighty one. I seemed to be dashing down the stairs, but in a second or two, found myself on the top landing again. I fought my way back, step by step, a score of times, down those stairs. I raced, scrambled, slithered, but in the end my will always won and I was back in safety, my head under the bedclothes.

A night came, however, when my will failed me and I was drawn across the threshold into that forbidden room. I found myself in utter darkness and a piercing shriek must have echoed throughout the whole house, for in an instant my father was rushing up the stairs. I was really there in the room because I had walked in my sleep. But that defeat or dividing of the will proved in itself a victory: the shock broke the spell and I was no longer summoned at night by the man called Shakespeare.

It was not until long afterwards that I discovered the secret of the picture. Art critics tell us that occasionally when the nose and other features in a portrait are out of drawing or insufficiently emphasized, the attention of the spectator is directed immediately towards the eyes and this optical illusion occurs. The effect seems to have been discovered in the Byzantine period and became so well known in the Middle Ages that it was used by religious painters for purposes of religious edification. Nicholas of Cusa refers to the novelty and in his tract, *De visione Dei*, set down in the latter half of the fifteenth century, describes a picture of this kind;

> Place it anywhere, say on the north wall of your Oratory; stand before it in a half-circle, not too close, and look at it. It will seem to each of you, whatever the position from which he looks, that it is as if he, and he alone, were being looked at. ... Then let a brother, fixing his gaze upon the icon, move towards the west, and he will find that the glance of the icon moves ever with him; nor will it leave him if he returns to the east. He will marvel then at this motion without locomotion.

Such spiritual exercises were not mine, and I fancy that the lay picture which afflicted me in childhood was but a freakish copy made by a careless or indifferent painter. It gave me a bewildering sense of guiltiness, but that was all.

II

When we grow up, we learn to control our fears and, in doing so, can often borrow unsuspected gifts from them. Many years later that upper room was to prove a refuge from alarms and excursions of a very different kind. Fear is certainly dramatic and that is why, unfortunately, the violence of war appeals to us despite ourselves.

Violence is rapid, though its results may last for generations; so the noise and ordered confusion, the rattle of lorries and armoured cars, disappear for a while until all that is furious comes back and war starts again. That is why I remember, as in a dream, the night when I sat in great misery, a solitary prisoner in a Black-and-Tan lorry instead of being in that room upstairs. It happened in this way. My family was residing at the time outside Dublin, but the house in which we had lived formerly was still unsold, and, for convenience sake, a chair and a stretcher bed had been left in that top back room. On this night I had been with a young woman writer, with whom I had fallen in love, and I had forgotten all about the curfew, for in those days of ambush, raid and reprisal, it is surprising how often the timid failed to notice the time. There was indeed no Tocsin or Curfew Bell to announce the hour when, all had to remain indoors: it came suddenly and there was a deathly silence in the streets. I had to reach the north side of the city without being arrested, and as it was quite late, I decided that it would look less suspicious if I kept to the main streets. Hurrying past the darkened houses, I could hear only the echo of my own footsteps. St. Stephen's Green was bright under the moon, the tram rails gleamed like the steel of bayonets, and beyond the electric standards were the wintry branches of the trees. But Grafton Street was full of shadowy shop-corners and I went cautiously in the middle of the road. So far I seemed to be the only late-goer that night and when, I got to College Green, I must have glanced at the clock above the gate of Trinity College, for I can remember clearly that it was almost midnight. I stood, listening for the ominous sound of lorries in the distance, but all was silent. As I hurried on, my hopes increased, but not for long; when I came towards O'Connell Bridge I saw the first patrol. Very humbly I approached the Officer in command and told him my tale of forgetfulness. He waved me sternly on and I felt that he was sending me towards my fate although O'Connell Street, as far as I could see, was quite empty. But when I got to Nelson Pillar I stopped again, for, at the corner of Earl Street, strolling up and down by himself, whistling cheerfully as he twisted an enormous Colt revolver, was an auxiliary. He was handsome, tall, his tam o' shanter set at a rakish angle and, despite my anxiety, I could not help admiring the recklessness of this midnight whistler. It seemed to me that, as he swaggered there, he was making of himself a deliberate draw for any sniper who chanced to be lurking in the shadows of the narrow street. So with a double fear in my mind, I came towards this young man whose mirth was more alarming than the sternness of the patrol at the Bridge. To my surprise, he nodded pleasantly, listened with sympathy, but told me that the main patrol might not let me pass. I turned and saw beyond the Pillar a lorry and nearby, about a dozen Black-and-Tans. I was halted, my excuses failed, and a squat truculent-looking fellow marched me over to the empty lorry. I climbed in and sat down, feeling that I was doomed. Frantically through my mind hurried all the stories of atrocities which I had heard of: I remembered only too well the newspaper accounts of prisoners shot while trying to escape and, like everyone else, I knew what that grim euphemism meant. I tried to think that my fears were exaggerated; that all would be well, that I would have to spend merely a few hours in a barrack cell. But it was in vain that I tried to deceive myself. The sentinel remained motionless beside the lorry; ten yards away the Black-and-Tans were standing with their loaded weapons. They scarcely moved: patiently and in silence they were waiting there for more victims. Mercilessly the minutes passed and then fear, as it chilled, brought me its last gift, a moment of poetic inspiration. I leaned over the side of the lorry and questioned my terrible guardian in a simple tone. 'Do you think there'd be a chance of a cup of tea when we get to the Barracks?' He looked up at me in amazement. Tea!' he exclaimed. 'Yes, I've not had a meal or anything for hours.' 'Neither have I,' he muttered gruffly. I expressed great sympathy with him and suddenly he began to tell me of his many grievances. At once we were human beings again and quite friendly with each other. 'I'll see what I can do for you' – he left me, and went over to the officer in charge. 'He says you can go,' said my deliverer, when he returned, 'but keep to the left of Rutland Square,' he added confidentially in his Lancashire accent which I have never forgotten; 'there may be another patrol on this side of it.'

Full of joy I hurried along, for in less than ten minutes I would be safe in the room which I had feared so much in childhood. Already in my imagination, as I turned the corner, I was watching the moonlight shining through the window, thinking with amusement of that strange oil painting which had seemed alive. I could see the sneer on his lips and those melancholy, accusing eyes.

Was it really a portrait of Shakespeare or of some unknown cavalier? And where had it vanished? Suddenly I heard a whisper. Someone was calling me in a cautious tone and I looked towards the dark alley on my left. A couple of young fellows, crouching in a doorway there, were beckoning to me excitedly. As they did so, I heard the clattering of footsteps and saw in the distance three Auxiliaries coming towards me in the middle of the road. Beyond them was a gloomy edifice known to all the children of the neighbourhood as the Black Church, and striding along between shadows and moonlight, these new enemies seemed even more formidable than those who had let me pass. My former home was only around the corner but it might have been in the next world. I felt that my luck had been too good to last and, to add to my difficulties, there was the problem of those two lads. As quietly and rapidly as I could, I murmured to them that they were liable to be shot at sight if they lurked there or ran down the lane, and so persuaded them to come with me. The Auxiliaries cuffed the pair and send them home to bed with a kick – but they let me pass less painfully

A few minutes later I had reached that empty house on the north side of the city. I fumbled with the latch door-key, then my hand was on the banisters, my foot on the stair. This time there was no struggle between my will and imagination, but I stopped to listen on the last lorry. Far away in the city I could hear the sound of shots. A moment later I was in the room upstairs.

Two

I

'THE rich blood of the Brownes!' exclaimed my mother one day as the bread-knife, which she was using, slipped and cut one of her fingers. In alarm I saw the large drop forming itself and turned away hastily to hide the emotion which overcame me. In that moment, I had realized for the first time our common blood and was aware of the many dead about whom I knew so little. I forgot how much I had raged secretly against her when I was growing up, our incessant quarrels over religion, my bitterness when she seized and burned those heretical books of mine, most of them in cheap reprints which I had to buy all over again. I knew, then, that I preferred that obstinacy of the Brownes, which was her pride, to the generosity and easy-going of my father. Her coldness and reserve would at last be mine also, and I saw clearly that it was her determination which had saved us all from indigence in the Liberties of Dublin long before I was born.

But in the years of adolescent mental struggle, I had felt motherless and carried my resentment into the next world, so that to this day I dislike the hyperdulia which is increasing in town and country. I did not realize how deeply I felt that growing loss until I was in my twenties and was dangerously ill in body and mind. For months I existed in a visional state which was heightened by the usual opiates. In a continual dream-sequence I followed the exploits of a Republican fighter in Limerick and the southern counties and at times his breathless escapes seemed mine. Other visions were eastern and I can remember countless Jewish children hurrying at nightfall through an immense gateway into a garden, so exquisite was the olive-and-ivory of their faces. One day I awoke in hot summer sunshine and, looking down the ward, noticed that the head of the patient in the last bed, on the right, was on the pillow beside him. I watched for a long time that strange sight, believing that I was suffering from all illusion, but the head with its closed eyes and short beard remained several inches away from the man's body. In my confused state of mind, I felt sure that he was St. John the Baptist.

When I dozed again, I was back in childhood and only separated from it by a feeling of intense grief. I was in the kitchen of our house in Mountjoy Street near the window which I had known so well. Every day from that window, I could see the concrete yard and shed, the tall swing, the elder bushes in the small garden, and beyond them the backyards of the cottages in St. Mary's Place. Paradise Lane was hidden by the walls and I could only see near the sky the backs of the tenements in Dorset Street, gay with washing hung from poles stuck out from the broken and patched windows. But it was evening now and the garden was greyer. I was beside the sewing machine and my mother had stopped the treadle. I was repeating to her my first prayer because my father had promised me sixpence if I could say it when he came back to tea and I was eager to gain the reward. Already I knew that he had left the Waste Water Department in Castle Street, near the City Hall, and was cycling down Parliament Street, across Capel Street Bridge, up Bolton Street, past the Fire Brigade Station, and, at any moment, I would hear his latchkey turn in the hall-door lock.

My mother's sudden exclamation that day reminded me of those early years in our Mountjoy Street home. Once a month, on Sunday, a bottle of stout appeared on the table when the cloth had been laid for the midday meal. Wrapping a napkin carefully around the nape, my mother drew the cork. Always I watched the small rite with interest, for I knew, then, that Grandfather Browne was coming. But the solitary black bottle with the tawny label, which had a harp on it, seemed to me in some obscure way a sign of evil. There was a mystery about my grandfather and I knew that he was in disgrace. This was all the more surprising because he was so venerable in appearance, having a long white beard, small, pale blue eyes, a lofty brow and bald top. He spoke in a gentle way, and seemed to be in awe of my mother. Often my sister Kathleen had told me that when she was smaller than I was at the time, he used to take her on his knee and make her promise that she would never become a nun. Despite his gentle wickedness, I gazed up at him with respect. Long ago he used to meet with other Fenian conspirators in the loft of a grain-store in Thomas Street where Lord Edward Fitzgerald had been arrested by the cruel Major Sirr at the beginning of the century. Beyond that, was a further past of his and I was well aware of it, for in our narrow hall there was a portrait of him in a heavy gilded frame as a lad beside his pony. On the opposite wall was another of my great-grandmother, Ellen Dardis of Meath. These old oil paintings, together with the pedestal on which was a bust of Napoleon bought by my mother at one of the auctions to which she hastened so often, gave grandeur to the gloomy hall, not to speak of the pheasant on the ledge of the fanlight. But this grandeur was not much compared with the display in the parlour, with its large cabinet, painted fire-screen, and the piano on which my eldest sister played, long before I was taught the violin. Here, too, was a glass chandelier, from which I was given a few broken prisms that concealed triangular sevenfold glories. On Sunday when the fire was glowing in the parlour, and the incandescent mantles were lit, the chandelier was a-dazzle. I owe to it my first moment of identity, for when I was held up to it as an infant, I twinkled into consciousness of a self.

The disgrace in which my grandfather lived must have had an influence upon me, for in secret I knew that I was deserving of the same treatment. It was comforting to find that so venerable a man could be as wicked as I was for somehow that seemed to disprove the stern morality of our family life. Truth to tell, I was guilty of all the little acts of curiosity about myself and others which have been set down by Freud and are denied with such vehemence by those who insist on the perfect innocence of childhood. Had I known that we cannot sin until the age of seven, which theologians hold to be the age of reason and consent, I might have been spared much anxiety and have rejoiced in my desire for knowledge. My mother was not, indeed, a religious fanatic or a ceaseless church-goer, indeed she was obeying an old Dublin custom when she refused to invite especially any clergyman to the house. But she had that stern Victorian sense of duty which spread to our country in the second half of the last century. So rare, so refined was this sense of morality which my sisters and I drew from her example, that, in comparison with it, the religion of the churches we attended seemed gross. In consequence it was at Mass that I got my earliest intimations of immorality, for the language of religion belonged to franker centuries. It was mainly through some of the scriptural texts which the priest read out in the short sermon on Sunday that I became conscious of the restraint in our own home life. I remember clearly my feelings of horror – as if I had some hereditary knowledge of forbidden things – when I heard for the first time *Matthew* 9.20. Because of this moral delicacy, even our family prayers became an ordeal which grew worse with every year. We said the Rosary each evening and when my Mother gave out the first half of the *Hail Mary* to which we said the response, her voice always changed as she came to the last words, 'And blessed is the fruit of thy Womb, Jesus.' The pace quickened and she ran them together. When, in turn, we said them, we imitated her rapid sing-song. The sentence was completely incomprehensible to me, but I suspected that it was improper, although it had been first spoken by the Angel Gabriel.

Strangely enough I enjoyed another experience which is usually reserved for little Protestants. Before I could spell out my letters I used to turn the heavy pages of our family Bible and, needless to say, it was the Douai version. I suspect that the illustrations in it must have been by Gustave Doré, so copious were they. Many of those I enjoyed were horrible depictions of battles, flights, torture and execution. I can still see that huge captive in one of them, tied down to a trestle, his limbs being chopped off with blades. But there was a full page plate to which I constantly turned, peepingly, for it was always there waiting for my shocked glance. It displayed a group of unclad fathers and mothers with their children clinging to rock or branch as the waters of the Flood rose towards them. Turning from it, I sought the pictures of fire descending from Heaven on false altars and the ground opening to swallow the wicked. I was dealing with something which was quite near. For, one Sunday morning after Mass, my sisters and I went down to the railings of Rutland Square to see the charred remains of the vast marquee which had been destroyed the night before by a stroke of lightning. Within it had been the Swiss Village, as it was called, this being a panoramic model of the Alps and their valleys. We knew that God sent fire from Heaven because the Exhibition had been open on the previous Sunday. Something of Puritanic feeling must have lingered in our neighbourhood for Sunday is now a day of enjoyment in Greater Dublin. During twelve o'clock Mass, the cycles are stacked outside the city churches and the ecclesiastical car parks beside the new churches in the surburbs are glassy with expensive motor-cars. But at evening thousands of these worshippers hurry to the cinemas, some of which are larger than the chapels.

Fear, too, ran along our street one week, past the shops, the old Victorian houses, the Protestant church, the terrace of brick houses, all the way down to the slum of Dominick Street, where an epidemic of smallpox broke out and we were hastily vaccinated.

On that Sunday, every month, both the bottle of Guinness and Grandfather Browne seemed to emerge from nowhere. I knew that he had become poor and was part-time secretary of the Ancient Order of Foresters. The bold Sean O'Casey, last defender of our lay liberties, has mocked at the Foresters. He has despised their green coats, white riding breeches and black top-boots, but it was a patriotic joy for us children to try and count several hundred Robert Emmets marching past. Often we watched the Home Rule processions from a window in Capel Street, where my first love, little Theresa, lived with her father and mother above a shop. She died when she was eight and I composed a dire little lament on the piano which I played often for our visitors. The bass consisted of a horrible succession of diminished fifths. Leaning over the window-box, my darling shook her ringlets as we watched bowler hats and sequin bonnets below, the immense banners of the trade unions, the crowded waggonettes, floats and drays with all their horses, heard the narrowing cheers, burst after burst, as the fife-and-drum bands and the marching men came nearer.

II

I fancied that the fall of my grandfather from grace had something to do with old Bishop Browne, whose name was familiar to me for I had heard it often. According to family legend, he was an ancestor of ours and had burned the National Relic of Ireland. This heirloom was known as the Bachall Iosa and is noted in the Annals of the Four Masters: 'The staff of Jesus which was in Dublin performing miracles from the time of Patrick to that time and which was in the hand of Christ when he was among men.' We are told, too, in the *Trias Thaumaturga* that it was enclosed in gold case made by Tassachus, the saint's goldsmith. George Browne has left a name of obloquy owing to that iconoclastic act, and recent historians have added to his shame in order to conceal the remarkable fact that during the reign of Henry VIII, all the members of the Hierarchy in Ireland, with two exceptions, renounced papal authority – though most of them were native – in order to save their temporalities. Of the early life of this English Bishop little is known except the fact that he was an Austin clerk. He was a friend of Thomas Cromwell and eventually became Master General of the religious houses in England and is said to have celebrated the marriage between the King and Anne Boleyn. In the year 1538 he was sent over to Dublin where he was enthroned as Archbishop and became active in reform. He has been denied sincerity, yet his enemies admit that he was interested in the devotional use of the Irish language, collected many ancient manuscripts and set down his plans for a great University of Saint Patrick. However, on the accession of the Catholic Queen Mary, he was deprived of his See. So the reformer and iconoclast disappears from history with his wife and children. The older ceremonies were restored, ceremonies which his subordinate, Bishop Bale of Ossory, described as 'the apes and toys of anti-Christ, the bowings and beckings, kneeling, and knocking.'

The place where Archbishop Browne burned the staff was Skinners' Row outside Christchurch Cathedral – in the very year he came over to Dublin. All seemed conclusive to me, for I knew that my great-grandfather, Henry Browne, and my grandfather had been skinners in Watling Street which is not far from the spot of desecration.

In later years, my mother remained silent about her own early life and it seemed almost as if she had forgotten or dismissed it from her memory. Sometimes, however, she would speak to me of her own grandfather, Henry Browne, whom she had never seen, and I felt that he had been a legend to her long ago. Although the tanning industry was slowly declining owing to the export of live cattle to England, he was well-to-do and, following a lively Georgian custom, went over with his wife in style every year to Newmarket or other race meetings. He was eccentric in his later years, wore a wig of different colour every second day of the week, and had built at the back of his tannery in Watling Street, a tower for study, which was still known in my mother's childhood as Browne's Folly. Great-grandfather used to compose satiric ballads about other merchants with whom he had quarrelled, have them printed as broadsheets, and sung by a ballad-maker outside their premises in Thomas Street and the neighbourhood. She remembered a few lines of one, but they have escaped my mind for ever.

As a child, I knew Watling Street well, for twice a year, my sisters brought me with them to the store nearby in Thomas Street, where they bought a stone of salt for a large wooden seller at home; and there were many ways by which we could reach that ancient part of the city, with, its stalls, its big and little shops. Sometimes we went underneath the last part of the old town-wall, by the fourteenth-century tower of St. Audeon's, and by the distillery. We passed Francis Street where our poor relatives lived in rooms, came down Watling Street or under the arch of Winetavern Street to the Quays again.

Many of these old hilly streets are changing and new working-men's flats have been built along them. The Guinness Brewery has long since spread on its monstrous way; vast offices of Victorian ugliness replaced the houses of James's Street, in one of which my mother was born; all day there is the sound of machinery, clanking small trains, and escaping steam. But at evening all is still. Recently I walked through the slums, clearances, tumble- downs of Pimlico, from which I could see, at every turn, the Dublin Mountains, went down shadowy lanes under the walls of the brewery which seemed a mighty stronghold of gain. Suddenly above a queer structure like a ziggurat, I saw a wisp of hot vapour rising with religious persistency, and thought how the prophets of the Chosen Race had railed against the worship of the Gentiles.

An ignorant relative burned the family papers our grandfather kept in a small mahogany box, parchments over which he had pored so long in his old age. Only one document survives, a genealogical roll which came into my possession some years ago. I unrolled it in much curiosity. With a pencil and florin, he had traced sixty-two circles of the family descent and wrote within them so finely that I had to use a magnifying glass to read the forgotten names in faded ink. Having been trained by Jesuits from the age of seven, I am still unable to hold opinions with certainty and envy those who can trust in private judgment. I hoped to find the name and the century of the second turncoat in his family, the Browne who changed back to the older faith, the last of us to exercise private judgment. A rapid glance down the chart showed me the worst. The Brownes did not appear in the document until a late period, when Henry Browne of Watling Street, married Maria, daughter of George Patten of Belville in the South Liberties of Cork, a merchant, who was born in 1738 and died in 1811. The genealogical details concerned, therefore, the Pattens and it was clear that my grandfather was proud of those other Protestant people. He had written out, by way of preamble, their claim to be descended from a brother of William Patten of Waynflete in Lincolnshire, who became Bishop of Winchester in the reign of Henry VI, Lord Chancellor of England, and was founder of New College, Oxford. Pattens of Warrington in Lancashire settled in Co. Cavan, but I noticed with regret that some of the circles were empty or half filled and wondered over those which were full. Who was John Patten of Co. Cavan, a victim of the plague in 1645? He grew up through a period when the European struggle between the armies of the two religions rent our country. During his life-time, Red Hugh had defeated the fellow-countrymen of John Patten at the battle of the Yellow Ford and three months after the victory the captured English flag were hung provocatively in the Vatican. Why did the Pattens move into Drogheda some time before or after the massacre by Cromwellian troops? Dorcas Patten and her husband died there, and Townley Patten was born there in 1706. In the eighteenth century some Pattens had moved to Cork and an Emily Patten, there, married a Lieutenant Lestrange of a Bengal Regiment. To my horror, I discovered that her brother, William, had been a First Lieutenant in the City of Cork Militia, for this yeomanry suppressed with many atrocities the outbreak in Co. Kilkenny during the Rebellion of 1798.

Of the Clarkes I know nothing, except that my grandfather, Denis Clarke, came from Black Ditches at Blessington, in Co. Dublin, near Clarke's Hill. The family intermarried with the Byrnes of Wicklow. Perhaps in the 1798 revolt our hearts beat in both camps.

Examining the magnified circles, I shared my grandfather's last pleasure on earth, though the bastard science of genealogy can be disproved by the multiplication table. But it is an Irish pleasure in which the medieval scribes indulged, as Desmond MacCarthy, the critic, mentioned to me before he was knighted. We were on the top of a bus, that noon, passing the quadriga at the corner of St. James's Park, and he was discussing with a gapped smile the Norman keep in Co. Galway which W. B. Yeats had just bought for forty pounds in order to aggrandize his Muse.

As a child, I was held up to see Queen Victoria entering Dublin but can remember only the ornamental gateway which had been constructed at the confine of the city. Large families at that time had their own smaller past during her reign because so many children died in infancy. There were twelve of us, but Mary Esther or Doto, Eileen, Kathleen and myself were the only survivors, for that was the herodean era. The names of our dead were set down piously on the fly-leaf of the Douai Bible, Augustine, the second eldest, Alice, Frances, John Joseph, Maurice, Henry, Georgina. Louis. Perhaps these babes had become confused memories to my poor mother, all except Georgina, a beautiful child, who lived to the age of six, for a photograph of her was kept on the mantelpiece in the parlour. But I can remember the funeral day of Louis, who was younger than I and died at the age of two from swallowing a grape-stone. This explanation may have been only a warning, for I was so fond of black grapes that I wanted to be Pope when I grew up in order that I might pluck bunches of them in the garden of my palace. We were constantly aware of the presence of our little brothers and sisters watching us from Heaven, for we knew that God had taken them back so that they might live happily ever after.

I had even a tinier past of my own because every morning my sisters set out for school at the Convent of the Sisters of Charity in Manor Street, opposite the house in which I had been born. I was told that there was a great orchard behind the terrace and wanted to see it, but Manor Street was a good distance away, beyond Constitution Hill, the King's Inns and Blackhall Place; besides the apple trees had already been cut down, for the old market gardens of Dublin were fast disappearing.

Beside the convent were better-class houses, in one of which Seumas O'Sullivan lived with his grannie, but he had been brought away years before my swaddling. Manor Street, which is a continuation of Stonybatter (Gaelic, Bother: road), was in ancient times part of the highway from Tara of the Kings to Cuala in Leinster. I am glad to think that a couple of poets were dandled beside a road along which so many chariots had swayed.

One Sunday, the bottle of Guinness did not appear on the table. Soon afterwards I was aware vaguely of a quarrel among aunts. In the middle of overheard words, a sister whispered to me the dire offence of which our grandfather had been guilty. Some years before, he had married a widow who owned a fruitshop on Ormond Quay, near the corner at Capel Street Bridge. Had the medieval notion that second marriages are almost adulterous lingered in Dublin or had my mother and her two sisters been shocked because of loyalty to their own mother, Ellen Dardis of County Meath, who died when they were all young? I cannot tell. But as a result of that new dispute, the monthly bottle was never put on the table again.

Sometimes Kathleen and I, when we were sent on farther messages, would steal to the quayside shop, stare at the apples and oranges in the window, peep through the doorway. The second wife was behind the counter, but we never saw Grandfather Browne again. One day, dozing by the fireside with his family papers around him, he fell forward towards the bars. The papers escaped burning that time, but the poor old man never recovered from the shock.

Three

I

A LARGE book of sermons appeared every year during Holy Week on the parlour table at home. It was heavily bound in leather, and had gold edges, and the pages were curiously cool and waxen to the touch. I approached that book always with great reverence, for whenever I ventured to open it, there emanated from it the faint, unmistakable fragrance of Frankincense. That remote sweetness was a constant surprise and delight to me in childhood. There were solemn illustrations within that book and as I turned the thicker processional pages, I watched bishops passing by in purple, and cardinals in their ample folds of flame.

The book was symbolical, for every night during that week my parents disappeared to some holy place on the south side of Dublin called Mount Argus. The sermons which rang out there above the heads of the congregation must have been passionate, for something of their excitement communicated itself to us even at home. We were increasingly aware all that week of world-shaking events, from the Great War in Heaven to the Descent into Limbo.

But it was the foreign name of Mount Argus which fascinated me as if the acrid sweetness hidden in that volume of sermons had drifted from its thuribles. I longed to go there, and at last, on a summer's evening, we set out upon our pilgrimage. I was not disappointed. Scarcely had we left the tram and crossed to the kerb when we found ourselves outside a gateway. There was a small footbridge, within the gateway, over a stream. The stream seemed to come from nowhere and disappeared under ground again, and along it were floating two swans. But this was not Mount Argus. We left the little bridge and hurried past small houses and gardens. Through another lofty gateway of wrought iron an empty hearse came and its silver rails were glittering behind glass. Then we saw another gate and there, to my astonishment, was the subterraneous stream again and the two swans were once more calmly floating on it.

I can remember only vaguely the choir and the changing lights in the church at Mount Argus, because of a few moments of terror when I was lost in the grounds. It was all due to the strange tree. I had run to see those branches which were glowing with rich multitudinous small fruit. I stood in awe beneath its shade for it seemed to me that I was under the Tree of Life itself, and certainly the night-green leaves were sticky as if with syrup and very sweet smelling. Gradually I became aware that I was not alone: someone else was standing there, very still, within the shadow of the tree. The stranger was clad in long robes and was bearded. His silent brooding presence filled me with a chilly sense of evil. I knew only too well that the Adversary is accustomed to appear to us in the shape we least expect; and so in my dread I mistook a Passionist for the Devil himself. I could not stir from the spot. I could not even call out. Slowly the figure turned and smiled at me in a strange way. That was enough. With a gulp of terror, I fled from the spot. That experience must have taken only a few seconds, for when I reached my mother, the crowd was still outside the church and she had not even missed me.

As we explore our own small past imaginatively, we find the fears and joys of childhood have taken on new meanings for us. All has become legend – and symbols are waiting for us. Had I been many-eyed I could not have seen more at Mount Argus or forgotten so quickly. Yet years later, when in a succession of delirious dreams, I hurried for months along grim corridors, up and down dark treacherous stairways, in and out of the wards and closets of great institutions, I was always trying to remember something that I had forgotten. As I rushed, in dreams, through those institutions, full of miserable and thwarted souls, all of us in frenzy trying to escape, yet imprisoned as if within the horrible architectural fantasies of Piranesi – in which ingenuity is bolted and barred by itself – there came at last that distant consolation:

> Flight beyond flight, new stories flashed
> Or darkened with affliction
> Until the sweet choir of Mount Argus
> Was heard at every window,
> Was seen in every wing . . .

Ibsen, in one of his lyrics, gives us a definition of poetry which seems appropriate to our needs, more so than many of those well-known definitions which we borrow from the English critics to our confusion.

> Poetry – 'tis a Court
> Of Judgment on the soul.

Certainly, the influences which shape our imagination are as subtle as they are unexpected. I can remember that startling occasion when, a few doors down the street, I heard a terrible cry of doom. Surrounded by a small agitated crowd, the local green-grocer was declaring in a stricken voice that he was John the Baptist. Had he appeared clad only in rough skins, we could not have been more shocked by this breach of the religious decencies. The abrupt transition from the half-naked sunny saint in the stained-glass window, which I knew so well, to this drab figure was almost too great for thought. But the terrible sincerity of the greengrocer, the agony in his face and tone almost convinced me. I knew that prophets appeared suddenly and were always disbelieved at first. I felt that he might really be the Precursor. He went crying out from our midst, calling down fire and heavenly vengeance, and long after, I could hear that awful voice making its way along Paradise Lane. That laneway was at the back of our street and had perhaps once been called that name in derision by its long suffering inhabitants. But the irony had gone and the name might have been transcribed from what Thomas Kettle calls 'the secret scripture of the poor'. Next day our evangelist disappeared into one of those big institutions where so many of our religious enthusiasts find their way.

More puzzling in its implications and therefore more memorable to me was the sudden appearance of the Blue Monk in our neighbourhood. For one marvellous week he appeared daily in our streets followed by an excited but reverential crowd. Women wept, prayed, murmured in joy as they stooped to touch the hem of his garment and sometimes they cried out that they were cured of their ailments and aches. His face was pale, delicate and beautiful, and I can still remember the crisp curls around his small head. The inexpressible sweetness of his expression as he suffered all this interfering reverence melted my heart. Nor had I ever seen so lovely a robe as the rich blue one that he wore. All that week I searched the streets to see him passing by or to join the small wondering crowd. I was well acquainted, of course, with the miracles of the saints. But these miracles were far off in time and mostly took place on the Continent. Indeed the medieval age of miracle-working had sadly declined into the tiny favours for which we clamoured daily to the canonized. If a pin-cushion or a purse were mislaid, St. Anthony found it for us and it appeared mysteriously under the hand. The great centuries of thaumaturgy had been domesticated for us. But now the street outside was new again with wonder. We might be running down the hilly steps of Siena, following St. Francis de Sales around the narrow street corners of Dijon, or crossing a piazza in Padua. But it was not long until whisperings and rumour filled our neighbourhood. Some said boldly that the Blue Monk was an impostor and came from Liverpool. The very name of that city had a dismal ring, for we knew that the churches had to be barred and bolted there during the week-days in order to protect the chalices and metal cups from sectaries. But what saint could flourish if there were no persecution, ill-will and envy? On Sunday, however, denunciations rang from our pulpit at late Mass, and on Monday morning the Blue Monk had vanished. I was bewildered and lonely as I roamed through the drab streets, and remained unconsoled by the fervours of Luisa de Carvajal, the Blessed Juliana of Mont-Cornillon and other distant saints. I am still a little confused when I realize that I owe my first glimpse into the age of miracles to a mad grocer and a good-looking impostor in a blue robe. Must we explain by desire those centuries when saints could divert a river from its very bed, cause rocks to float, and watch chapels being transported through the air by angels? Was the human mind in some preparatory trance dreaming of the wonders to come, those scientific wonders which have proved so unpleasant in use?

Our preoccupation with the next world is surely fit subject for our poetry. But we still need complex forms which will reflect the intellectual excitement of the ages and our own earliest intimations. Certainly, as a child, I knew a great deal more about the next world than this one. The Adversary was so often at my elbow that, in fits of bad temper and self-will, I could feel reflected on my face the overwhelming heats of his presence. Chief among these physical contacts with the next world was one which may have been unorthodox but was strangely moving. A tiny ringing in the ear meant that a poor soul in Purgatory was crying to us for aid. Coming from a vast distance, that minute sound had lost all its terrifying agony, yet kept its urgency. Who could not fail to be flattered by that auricular appeal and moved by the pathos of its anonymity? All those self-attentions in the life-long quest of eternal pleasure, that fearful last-minute rush of the Irish consciousness into the waiting mould of repentance, and then that sad, ultimate namelessness! Even the names read out at Mass so quickly lessened into the Month's Mind and then disappeared altogether into a general Commemoration.

II

Outside the coal-shed there was a hollow in the concrete and when the April showers raced across the sky, rain-water collected there for a little while. The sun came out again, the elder bushes in the corner of our narrow garden were shiny; and that small pool outside the coal-shed gleamed by itself. A grown-up would not have noticed anything strange about it, and would have been too big to discover its secret. I cannot remember how I discovered the secret of the pool, but its appearance in the concrete had always been a surprise and mystery. A bit of sky had fallen there, for, a few minutes before, the rain-drops which formed it had been miles up in the air.

When I sat on a box just inside the coal-shed and looked down at the pool, there, in that half-inch of water, was a brighter hemisphere than the one on which I lived. Pointing downwards into the blue sky were the clustering housetops of a city and, deeper than the last windows and gable ends, were the shining leads, the pinnacles of a mighty church. The main spire of that church tapered so far down into the sky that I could not see the minute tip of the lightning conductor. However much I turned my head, I could only see less than a ward of that city; but it was easy to imagine all those other house-tops, spires and great buildings. The city was fair because I saw it at a distance: the slate roofs and chimneypots were new in the sunlight, and the church was of shining jet. I could not see the streets of that city as the house-tops were too close together, but I imagined those streets filled with blessed crowds for it seemed to me that this was the celestial city of which all spoke. I was not puzzled by the fact that the sky was underneath instead of above, and that the happy citizens must be walking upside down. The flies on the kitchen ceiling were always walking upside down and I considered it an enjoyable condition. It is easier to look down than to look up, so the people hurrying through those streets, which I could never see, must be always looking down into the depths of blue sky. When the pool had disappeared, I still watched the white clouds with peculiar interest, knowing that miles up in the sky were rain-drops which would come down, while the sun was hidden, and form that tiny speculum once more.

When I looked round me I saw an entirely different world. The backs of the houses were shabby with weather-worn plaster, water-pipes were bunched under the small bathroom windows in the top storeys. The roofs of sheds below had blobs of moss between their slates, the galvanized iron was rust-eaten, and, beyond the top-heavy creeper on the wall, a few backyards away, was the side of a gaunt Protestant church. The lancets of that church were dark and unlighted, for the sun never seemed to reach them. The greater and lesser spires, the long row of pinnacles, gleamed greyly when a ray touched them, but on wintry days they were black and looming. Because of its grim, forbidding appearance, this edifice was known locally as the Black Church, and the name, with all its theological implications, was apt.

The Black Church stood in a space to itself and there was a railing with spikes all round it. The doors were locked during week-days, and that surprised us as children, for our chapels were always open from seven o'clock in the morning. After school the little boys and girls from Paradise Lane, which was at the back of our street, scampered around the Black Church. But at night the shadowy gas-lit place was silent and deserted, except for the echoing footsteps of a passer-by or the rumble of a cab. As children, we were told that anyone who ran round the church three times after dark would meet the Devil himself on the third round, but none of us had the courage to test the legend. Always, when I came late at night with my parents from the south side of the city, it was an exciting experience to pass that terrible church in complete safety. As we hurried by, I thought of the secret pool and knew there was another hemisphere in which all is different. There the Black Church, which I feared so much when I looked at it, was radiant, lovely and enskied.

Nature cherishes the young as best it can and in my own case dispelled my fear of the Reformation by giving me the Antipodes for a plaything. A half-inch of rain-water outside a coal-shed had saved me from that *odium theologicum* which overshadows our childhood.

One Sunday morning, the unexpected happened. Two little Protestant girls had come from the south side of the city to spend the day with us. They called in for a few moments to tell us that they had to attend morning service first. I looked at them in wonder for I realized that they were actually going to the Black Church.

'Will you go with them or come to Mass with us?' exclaimed one of my sisters, laughing so much that I firmly believed that the Devil was at her elbow.

'He'll come with us,' said Tatna merrily.

'Yes, do!' Dinty hugged me in delight.

'You won't leave us, will you?'

'Of course he will. I know he'll come with us.'

In bewilderment I was swept into that happy mock-earnest game. I knew indeed that it was a dreadful sin to attend any place of Christian worship other than our own, but I was tempted by an irresistible curiosity. As I wavered among these happy voices, I saw that my parents were smiling too. Was it a test of infantile orthodoxy? Were my parents smiling merely to hide their anxiety? I was overcome by sadness, and then, with all the wilfulness of a child who has determined to greet the Devil, I exclaimed:

'I'll go with Tatna and Dinty!'

To my surprise, everyone laughed good-naturedly. Happy hands straightened my collar, pulled my bow aright, tidied my hair. In less time than it takes to tell, Tatna, Dinty and I were running across the street and up the steps of the Black Church.

As soon as we entered, I was filled with astonishment, for the interior of the church was as bright as its exterior was dark. I had only known the dimness of old city churches, the rich gleam of stained-glass windows in the transept with all their saints and instruments of torture. When I knelt behind great pillars, all was shadowy and mysterious, so that the suspended lamps seemed to be of rare silver and ruby as the clouds of incense rose, and even base metal was precious. But through the lancets of the Black Church came a plain and temperate daylight which showed all clearly.

The service had already begun and the church was filled with people. Tatna and Dinty walked straight up the middle of the nave and I followed them obediently. Just as they were entering their places, I paused – and then, with great solemnity, I genuflected before the simple altar. Scarcely had my knee touched the ground when I remembered the warning which one of my sisters had whispered in my ear as we left the house. Terror-stricken, I realized the mistake I had made, for, in the awful moment, it seemed to me that the whole congregation glared at me and that the very preacher had stopped in astonishment to point accusingly at the tiny idolater.

The shriek of victims put to the sword, the black-topped flames around the crackling stake, the penal laws – I might have known them all in those few seconds.

But the burden of Europe cannot be sustained for long by the young. With a gentle smile, Tatna caught my hand and squeezed it affectionately. Hundreds of people were singing in triumph and I hid my ignominy beneath their mighty hymn.

Four

I

WHEN I was in my early twenties, I visited Paris for the first time and met James Joyce there. I remember well the evening on which he told me dolefully that of all the thoroughfares of our native city he preferred Capel Street. He was recovering from a bad cold and had sent me a postcard, asking me to call at the flat which he and his wife had just rented, near or in the *Rue de l'Université*. I went in some trepidation for he had been anxious to see my first book of verse, published by the well-know firm of Maunsel in Dublin. I had sent home for a copy with some reluctance because I felt that a long narrative on a Gaelic story of elopement would be outside his interest. Moreover, I was aware that his eyes were troubling him. I suspected that he was curious; I knew he was kind. He had given me a loan of those copies of the *Little Review* in which chapters of *Ulysses* had appeared and felt no doubt, that I expected him to ask me.

On arriving at the flat, I found to my surprise that the invalid was not up yet. The moment I sat down beside the bolster, I was filled with embarrassment for I saw Miss White peeping at me immodestly from under the bed. (Unlike Yeats, I have but the euphemistic speech of my boyhood.) While I was wondering whether I could push back gently with my foot that disturber of my peace, I heard Joyce confessing, from a remote distance, that he had been unable to read my poem. I was put out by such frankness but not much depressed. Truth to tell, I did not care very much for his own *Chamber Music*, a slim volume which many regarded even then with reverence. Moreover, although I had not dared to tell him so, I was completely puzzled by the experimental method of *Ulysses* and knew the streets of Dublin too well to become excited over them. So I was content with my own excursions through more than a thousand years of Gaelic literature, a subject about which he was entirely ignorant. Unfortunately, therefore, when he mentioned Capel Street to me on that November evening, most of my thoughts went straying.

Soon after I had come back from Paris, I wrote a sketch about our Great Exile and I copy it out for you now because immediate impressions are usually of interest. I regret the entranced style and the youthful lack of due reverence.

II

'It had been his whim for the little time in Winter that I was acquainted with him to meet me in a dark narrow byway, lit only by gas and rain-pools, under the blank wall of Saint Sulpice and because, if I remember aright, of some story of Renan that seemed to me irrelevant or fantastic. Always at the turn of six of the clock he was there before me, a tall melancholy bearded figure in black overcoat, fretting, impatient, striding up and down beneath the holy wall or standing despondently at the kerb. It was our custom, so quickly does one fall in to usage, to cross the road-pools and go into a cheap cafe, where, amid a vague restless feeling of people, we sat in the great ponderous ring of silence that had been made by him, and, opposite, I sipped pale aniseed with disappointment, yet, since there was little else to do, lingeringly, as though it had been the absinthe of which he had spoken. What could I say to him? What could anybody say to him? I sat ill at ease as a small boy who has not courage to raise his hand in some eternal class held slackly by a dejected schoolmaster. The fact that I had been to the same school a generation after him and had known the same streets and people in later years occupied him and seemed to me fantastic and unreal. As he sat there gazing abstractedly through dim glaucous spectacles and sighing to himself, I was scarcely aware of him, for, in the intolerable circumstances of silence, a dismal force constrained my mind back to the past. The "Portrait of the Artist" had long since become confused with my own memories or had completed them and, set up by his recollecting presence, I heard, as in correspondence, the murmur of classes and chalk squealing on the blackboard until teeth cringed, saw the faces of boys that I had hated and Jesuits in black soutanes, the brass candlesticks turned upon some common lathe that had seemed to him like "the battered mail of angels", and, with heart in shoes, I waited, having had, as I fancied, those thoughts that are forbidden by the Sixth Commandment, for the fatal sound of the sliding panel of the confession box, until suddenly the tenuous voice of Dedalus broke the silence like falling glass – and Jesuits, boys, candlesticks and sins against the Blessed Virgin and all the abracadabra of childhood vanished down the trap-doors of the mind to lie in wait for the next dream or perilous temperature.

"Dublin," he was saying to me, "is the nearest city to the Continent. Places here in Paris on a Saturday night are like Capel Street and Thomas Street. There's the same joy and excitement, as though bargaining for Sunday's dinner was a holiday. The very faces I see seem to be the same."

It was clear from all he said that the grey capital had become for him that strange allegoric city from which Christian fled and yet that shining one of which the faithful desire to be good citizens. I saw him wandering the streets, watching for the visional faces he had known, analytic yet sentimentalist. A phase of sensitive early experience arrested, assuming the continuity of dream-existence, sharpened by the files of feverish memory, as when for a month the mind is stopped by disappointed love, and detail and light and the populated region between sleeping and waking are alive and morbidly fascinating, in terms like these, rightly or wrongly, I was aware of his mind. I felt, too, that he only spoke Italian in his own secluded life so that English, like his past, might become semi-objective, pure medium, with tangible noun or adjective; seriously as a schoolboy carving wood with a blunt penknife, I saw him making his sentence a day, yet into intricate shape. With a head full of romanticism, I thought it fantastic to recall the doings of schoolboys or those unpleasing rhymes which are passed around when the first down appears on the cheek. To tell, briefly, during the melancholy silence, of the ancient Liberties of Dublin, of Tenter's Fields now brick, of changing shops and repainted, or auctioned, public-houses – and regarding the latter I was unhappily at that time but ill-educated – was more pleasing, for it was his delight to test his memory of local detail, and as he never erred, his face remained lit with a faint enthusiasm.

"Is Mulvaney's shop still there at the corner?" he asked me so suddenly one evening that I was startled from reverie. I looked at him quickly, suspiciously, thinking, egotistically, that he had detected my secret thought: for I had been staring into that visionary shop-window at sweets, seditious newspapers and hurley-sticks, all green and beautiful in incandescent gas as the glass I was holding before the light. That shop, in feverish dreams, came usually before me, radiant as the last tram, but with more celestial glory, and it contained some mystical significance that I have never discovered. But Stephen Dedalus was deeper in his own memories and I saw that it was useless to confess to him and so the faint glow and gurgle of enthusiasm that prelude talk faded in me or quietened. I pretended, then, that I was alone, that I saw him going home, lessening down the Street of the Annunciation, by the Street of the Conception and disappearing from the ultimate Street of the Assumption, not quite regardless of those mysteries, yet thinking of the sentence that awaited him. I saw myself liberated from the mental circle of him and of the past, crossing the Boulevards and the moon perhaps like a silver franc in the sky. I saw through a cloud of tobacco smoke the diminished brightness of the Closerie des Lilas and Paul Fort, very neat as a Huguenot clergyman, and I anticipated the two words that the Prince of Poets would give me as I sat down among the young men drinking black coffee and cognac.

By that time, we had got up in silence, and come out to the kerb and, with a word and a sigh, Stephen Dedalus had gone into the night.'

III

Only recently have I found that Capel Street meant much to me when I still went bare-kneed. All the way from Drumcondra, through Upper and Lower Dorset Street and Bolton Street, that thoroughfare kept changing its name, becoming Capel Street as far as Grattan Bridge, renaming itself Parliament Street for a short distance and ending not ingloriously at the City Hall. Along the left-hand side of Capel Street which had several sweetshops, my sister Eileen and I walked slowly during a few weeks for I had hired her as my storyteller before I could read very well. The rate was sixpence for twenty fairy-tales, but I must have been able to count because I insisted on getting full value for my money and the transaction was never repeated. In Capel Street, too, lived Theresa O'Doherty, who was as lovely as Kathleen, although her ringlets were black and not of gold like my sister's. Later I hurried every week down to the dark little music shop on the right-hand side of that thoroughfare, so often did the E string of my violin snap, so hard did I practise. As a student, I came back to the Municipal library there and among its grimy books found the *Deirdre Wed* of the neglected Irish poet Herbert Trench and imitated it in that first long poem of mine which James Joyce could not read.

One night, therefore, I decided to revisit Capel Street and, passing by the long, patient queues outside the cinemas in O'Connell Street, came to Parnell Street, which was known in less patriotic days as Great Britain Street. I turned around the second corner into Dominick Street where the Georgian mansions have been tenements for three-quarters of a century or more: now they have been condemned by the Corporation, being in too bad a state to be saved. The street was ill-lit and shadowy: even the youngsters from the laneways nearby seemed to have abandoned it. A watchman was huddled beside his brazier, and I could make out behind scaffolding poles and protective hoarding the semi-ruins. A dead street for the time being, windows concreted, floors ripped, sudden gaps of basement. A few of the tenements were still inhabited and I stared at a ground-floor window with a feeble greenish light within, perhaps from a broken gas mantle; cardboard patches against a few of the broken panes, the door wide open, the hallway pitch-black and ill-smelling. But at the far end of Dominick Street some of those noble houses are well preserved. Shining like a good deed in that naughty world, despite its sad name, was Dolorosa House, the Legion of Mary Youth Centre. Beside it was another shabby tenement with a shattered fanlight. But the next three doors were as finely grained and varnished as in the past. There the Sisters of the Holy Faith have a Private School, to which I went for a week. But I was already beyond the infant class, for I could read Aesop's fable of the Fox and the Grapes, which had a dim papal significance for me, and so I was taken away front the smiles of the holy dames.

On the opposite side of the road is St. Saviour's Church and I hurried in by one of the swing doors. The dim religious twilight which I had known in childhood as I knelt behind the great pillars was gone and I tiptoed into the bare glory of concealed fluorescent lighting. In the nave were sodality women, all respectable and most of them elderly. Along the aisle, where I hesitated, a few aged men were kneeling. Out of a loudspeaker, high among the arches, came a huge voice:

'... and we must intercede with the Mother of God, Mary, Queen of Heaven...'

I glanced at the large new statue in white-and-gold of the Blessed Virgin on a lofty pedestal in front of one of the pillars at the top of the nave. As I could not see the pulpit, I wondered whether the voice was being relayed, for I have been told that in some churches the Rosary is given out at evening from a record played in the vestry by the clerk. After a few minutes, however, I saw the preacher rapidly coming down the spiral stairway which led into the aisle, his black cloak and cream habit aswirl. As he descended, soft organ music was filling the church and at the same time, in white-and-gold cope and robes, the celebrant with his servers swept silently towards the crimson-carpeted steps of the High Altar, where already the candles in the brass sconces were lit for the Benediction, and of a sudden the music rose to a full crescendo.

I glanced furtively at the titles of the pamphlets in the glass case on the wall near me. The booklets about the saints, their wonderful lives and miracles, were no longer there to delight the young. Instead I saw the battle-array of religious action: *Communism and the Home* by Douglas Hyde, a recent English convert and lecturer, almost better known nowadays than his Protestant namesake who translated the *Love Songs of Connaught* and became first President of our country, *Christian Science*, an exposure by another English convert, Monseigneur Knox, and other bellicose covers were in that row among sundry liturgical tracts and explanations of the new evening Masses for businessmen. *Penser! Nos convertis feront cela pour nous.*

On coming out from the church, I turned with expectancy, hoping to see the small repository which I had known so well.

But the house and shop were a condemned, tumbled-down ruin. I turned away quickly, remembering the simple treasures on which we gazed, although there were no religious music-boxes then, or filament complete with electric plug. We had, for handling, beads of red cut-glass or amethyst, slender chain, metal crucifix with toylike figure too small to suffer any pain, the swimming gleam of expensive mother-of-pearl beads for best use, thick and thin rosaries in blue, white and Franciscan brown. Only later came those gross beads of Irish cowhorn specially manufactured by a Protestant firm to flatter rural fingers.

I hurried around the corner of Dorset Street to see the Priory and garden, always so dark at night behind the high railing. As children, we passed by in awe for we knew that the monks were wrapped in contemplation or praying for all of us. But to my astonishment the building was new again and had many lighted windows. On the opposite side of the road near the public house was Long Lane, down which I had often run on messages from Mountjoy Street. Leaning against a wall was an elderly man with shabby coat and a cap which might have belonged to Sean O'Casey forty years ago. I crossed over to him, explained that I had not been in the district for some years and asked him whether the Priory had been rebuilt. Seeing my large black hat and overcoat, he came to the other kerb, eager to tell me all I wanted to know.

'That's the new extension, Father. Here at this end. It was done two years ago.'

I murmured that I was only a layman, but he was too intent to pay heed to what I said.

'And there's more new building going on at the back, Father, and they're going to concrete the garden.'

He pointed to the window of a lecture-room in the semi-basement.

'That's the Catholic Boy Scouts Clubroom, Father.'

Looking down between the railings, I could see boys in a row, listening, with serious faces.

'And that's the Women's Whist Club up there. Most of them will be round in a few minutes from Devotions. And there's a fine hall inside, Father, full of people. You could go in now, Father, if you like and one of the Fathers would be only too glad to show you round. But it would be better to come in the morning, Father, when you could see the new buildings at the back. And now come with me, Father, and I'll show you the lamb.'

Puzzled by his remark, I followed him obediently.

We stood before a handsome new entrance over which the

medieval emblem of the Holy Lamb was cut finely in the granite.

'The clergy used to use the old entrance in the back lane before the alterations were made.'

He glanced to the left.

'And I suppose you remember that, Father?' He paused and lowered his voice.

There, indeed, beside the Priory, was the eighteenth-century house with the plaque to Richard Brinsley Sheridan.

'Mr. and Mrs. Vernon used to live there until recently. I'm sure you remember him, Father. He has a slight halt. The house has been taken now by a doctor . . . you wouldn't know him, Father. But you must come again tomorrow, Father, and you'll be able to see the whole place better in the daylight, Father.'

While he was talking, I fumbled in my pocket and found that I had, in change, the price of a pint. I explained that I was in a hurry, promised to come back in the morning and begged him to drink my health in the pub over the road. I saw him start ever so slightly and I read his eye: he knew that I had seen through his excessive little act. His tone changed, and as one layman to another, he thanked me simply and left, thank Heaven, without tipping that cap which Sean O'Casey might have worn forty years ago.

I am used to being mistaken for a priest and so I am no longer embarrassed by the respect paid to my cloth. As a provincial youth, ignorant of new literary ways, I believed that a poet must wear a wide-brimmed black hat and grave suit. Sometimes as I cycled along country roads, I was saluted by carter or stone-breaker, so I consulted a clerical student, who was an intimate friend of mine. He told me what to do in order to spare the feelings of passers-by who might salute me. For a year or so after his ordination, a young priest always raises his hat; gradually he learns only to touch it; then he moves his hand only as far as his shoulder – and at last a mere showing of his right palm suffices. With the increasing ruralizing of Dublin and the spread of religious action since the Civil War, my hand is kept busy. In particular, the Cork men who live here now are a daily problem. When they are in a bus, they spend much time raising their hats, or if they are bare-headed, crossing themselves as ostentatiously as possible, not only at every church we pass but at unseen oratories and private chapels in convents, orphanages, colleges, Magdalen Homes, hospitals and industrial schools, some of them not less than a quarter of a mile away. When they get off the bus, they seem to be looking around for the nearest clergyman to reverence. Frequently, therefore, as I walk along the city streets, I am saluted, and in the suburbs, motorists, lorry-drivers, cyclists and small boys pay me undue respect. Clergymen on their autocycles give me a professional nod, or glance at me quickly, as they come out of the cinemas in the afternoon. Sometimes I am tempted to take vicarious advantage of my old-fashioned poetic garb. When I draw my black muffler closer to hide my lack of celluloid collar, I am offered a seat immediately in an over-crowded bus, receive attention in tea-shops, quicker sherries in the larger hotels – and I need never wait more than a few seconds outside a telephone booth.

IV

As I came towards Capel Street, memories were jumping over counters, and bounding out of shops that had changed their owners long since or had gone down in the world. Most of our family provisions came from Murphy's of St. Mary's Abbey, a turning near the far end of Capel street, and we often went there on extra messages, calling on the way back, perhaps, to Fenelly's at the corner of Dominick Street for candles, colza oil, or the paraffin tin which we had left there to be filled. We passed by King's Inn Street, where Uncle John had his hackney premises opposite the large convent and school.Under a gateway, we crossed the cobbled yard through an odour of straw, to the parlour. There we got lemon pudding and other delicacies which Aunt Ciss learned to make in New York, where Uncle John and she had met many years before as immigrants. Sometimes I went down King's Inn Street slowly, savouring the smell of Barrington's soapworks, which became so powerful at last that the sunny round of sky seemed a vast galvanized bath of suds. It was always Monday down that street, always washing-day.

Over the road I could see with my mind's-eye the toyshop where Mrs. O'Carroll and her daughter Babbie had scarcely elbow-room to serve us. But the many-coloured window of Barry's sweetshop was dusty and I found myself staring at a few pitiable objects. Mr.

Barry seemed to us almost a magician, for he boiled the sweets he sold, but he rarely emerged from all that hidden sugariness, those thickenings, skimmings and ladlings of his. One day I went in to buy some liquorice allsorts and came out with one of those inspired remarks which become family sayings and are perhaps the origin of all proverbs. Mr. Barry's proud and fair-haired little daughter, who was about my own age, was talking behind the counter to the shop girl. With a contemptuous toss of her plaits, she glanced at me, ceased her confidences and said in a loud tone:

'Wait till *that* goes out!'

Indignation bore me home with the little brat's remark, which lasted for many years and was used aptly on many occasions. Another useful remark was made by a small boy belonging to the Hannigan family, who came from Tipperary and owned the grocery shop and Off Licence beside our house. One day there was a bowl of apples on the kitchen dresser. Paddy stopped at the door, staring at it with bigger eyes, and announced:

'I shmell apples!'

This seemed to us the very top of rustic cuteness and simplicity. Curiously enough our neighbours in the dairy shop on the other side also came from the country. The McKeon girls were large and handsome, rounded as the cream crocks, milk cans and churns among which they moved. Their looks were bold but no more, and this was puzzling to us, for they came from Banagher and there is a well-known proverb – 'That beats Banagher and Banagher beats the Devil.' Once a week there was a rush of hoofs, as cattle were driven under the archway beside the dairy to the long sheds of brown galvanized iron. At night there were country sounds all around us, faint bellowings, and far away the whistling of goods-trains going back to the Midlands. But the next morning the cattle were already in the market-fairs at Prussia Street, long before we were awake. Often we laughed over country credulity. Our parents told us, for instance, how a few practical jokers had flashed a lantern-slide on a white-washed gable in a County Mayo village and the astonished natives believed that they beheld a vision of the Blessed Virgin. But our Dublin mirth seen to have been in poor taste, for there is now a great annual pilgrimage to the village of Knock, eminent doctors attend, and hundreds of invalids are brought by train to be cured of their afflictions. Nevertheless my city doubts come back to me whenever I read of the latest cures. Some years ago a woman journalist told me how she had been sent down to Knock to write an article about the pilgrimage. The villagers tried to prevent her from meeting the oldest inhabitant, who was, they assured her, slightly 'touched'. Her curiosity was aroused and she succeeded at last in tracking down the only survivor of the youngsters who had witnessed the wonderful vision in the 'eighties' of the last century. The results of her interview with him, never appeared in print.

Beyond Barry's Sweetshop was another firm of the same name. Here I was measured for my boots, and they were made of leather as stout, I am sure, as that which came long ago from my great-grandfather's tannery. Every boy at that time had metal protectors and studs which brightened the more he ran. The tram-tracks which bore the Ballybough tram down Capel Street are gone, and I stopped at the corner to think of the pins I had often put on a track when Macaulay's *Lays of Ancient Rome* were sounding in my head. After a tram had passed, the common pin had become a perfect short blade for a tiny legionary.

Whether we went down Capel Street around by Green Street Courthouse or by City Market, we came inevitably to Murphy's of Mary's Abbey. Our mother bought there the best Danish bacon, butter and eggs in winter, and in summer the best Irish bacon, butter and eggs. It was a large, draughty shop but behind it was a smoke-house, with glowing ashwood and almost hidden in the gloom above hung the Limerick hams. Our grandmother had become a customer at Murphy's on the very first day the shop opened, more than a century ago. On coming back from London to live in Dublin, I tried to renew that family custom. The vanman called around to us at Templeogue on his way to a large and wealthy religious institution at Rathfarnham – with our modest ration of rashers, butter and eggs, an odd cut of ham, an occasional boiling fowl. A few pence were always knocked off, but as the bills were quarterly and we feared credit, my wife and I had to end that tradition of more than a century.

Musing outside the wholesaler's, I thought of the Christmas turkey, weighed and trussed for us there. Not least among the wonders of Christmas was the automatic jack which was wound only once a year. Now and then, I took my turn with the long iron spoon and basted the great hen revolving slowly in front of the kitchen range. That day is the longest in the year, for all fortunate children wake at six o'clock in the morning and, awed by that unearthly hour, grope towards the unknown joys at the end of the rail. My bed was in a corner of the large front room on the first floor, and when the venetian blinds were only half-drawn at night, I could see the glimmer of the street lamp. On a press by the mantelpiece was a shrine with a glass bowl of colza oil, on which a minute light was afloat, the wick being in a tiny holder of tin and soaking wood. That thick oil was used in the sanctuary lamp, and we believed that the chapel clerk would be guilty of sacrilege should he forget to renew it in time. By that holy flame so near me, it was a delight, while my parents were still asleep, to sit up and handle those half-seen gifts which had come from another world. The faithful must have felt as exalted in past centuries when sudden blooms were presented to them in wintertime or other supernatural objects by a heavenly messenger. In a few years, however, come the first doubts. Like all children, I discovered the deception too soon, when I came upon a toy gun hidden in the hot cylinder press some weeks before Christmas. I said nothing and fingered its trigger on that holy morning.

As I left Mary's Abbey, I realized that I had forgotten all about the violin shop, so completely had my subconscious abandoned music for poetry. I retraced my steps and found that it was still there, but in the window were saxophone and popular song-sheets, where, austerely, in the past, had been a couple of violins and round boxes of resin. I thought of Mr. O'Neill, who was tall, pale and melancholy, with long white hair asweep, very like the picture of composers of my music book-covers. His brother, who was stout, low-sized and bald, was usually in the workshop, but he came out sometimes to serve when the door-bell rang. With a shiver I recalled that early discipline of scales and what James Stephens has called 'strict joy'. Certainly I loved the delicate silken E string, but the A and D strings were rather common, as yellow, when they were new, as the washing-soap made by Barrington's. But I knew delight when, for the first time, I advanced from a copper G string to a silver one. How often, too, I glided upward to the fifth and sixth position or from below, with lighter touch, sped beyond them to the faint region of harmonics. There were minute angelic notes near the bridge, but beyond its frets were discord and disillusion.

As I turned from the music-shop and went towards Capel Street Bridge, rain was beginning to close in around me and Parliament Street was so dim that I could scarcely see Tormey's Bar to which my father and Mr. Corr, his clerk, were wont to adjourn. Beyond was the large pedestal outside the City Hall on which once stood the statue of the Liberator, Dad of Catholic Emancipation.

Often I had gone towards the bridge to watch the Guinness barges lower their funnels, and dashed across from one cloud of smoke to be enveloped in the other on the opposite side. Suddenly I remembered the last time that Kathleen and I had stolen down Capel Street towards the forbidden fruitshop on Ormond Quay in the hope of seeing Grandfather Browne once more. As we came by Lemass's hat-shop, some people were gathering at the corner. We hurried forward to see a redcoat regiment marching down from the barracks near Kingsbridge and the Infirmary Road, where old Mrs. Thunder lived. Then we heard the clatter of hoofs and knew at once that the Lord Lieutenant of Ireland and his escort were coming. Once we had been to a garden party at the Viceregal Lodge, for the higher Corporation officials were invited there in those days of entertainment. My sister ate so much ice-cream in one of the marquees that she got sick, but I have forgotten all about our visit. We were just in time to see the lesser might of the British Empire pass by on that sunny afternoon: the Earl of Dudley in his carriage, with all his outriders and prancers.

I would like to think that the exact date was June 16th, 1904, but a poet, who has been acquainted with the Society of Jesus too soon, can never be certain of anything in this world.

V

The trams passed by the far end of Mountjoy Street every few minutes on their way to the Phoenix Park and the Botanic Gardens at Glasnevin. As the front of them was open, the drivers could be seen moving their brass levers controlling the wonderful current of electricity, which sometimes spluttered in bad temper from the top of the trolley. On wet days they glistened in tarpaulins as they slowed down their lightning, the rain coursing down their cheeks, thickening their whiskers and streaming over their leather gloves.

A few steps took us to Berkeley Road Chapel, where we went usually, on Sunday, to eleven o'clock Mass. In the grounds were small rockeries and winding paths along which I walked in the May processions, the only surviving boy of our large family, clad proudly, as the other saintlings, in white surplice and black soutane, attentive to the medieval mysteries. Beyond the church was a triangular plot, opposite the Mater Misericordiae Hospital, and behind its railings was a memorial to the Four Masters, annalists of ancient Ireland. But we had to hurry past the small terraces on the opposite side with their many turnings, for in a corner shop, Mr. Lowry, the little tailor, had gone suddenly out of his mind and cut his wife's throat. The last shrieks of the poor, bloodied victim were still there.

Through the Church grounds we could reach Eccles Street, with its lofty Georgian houses, but much of it was too respectable to be interesting to us, for no children chalked their happenings on the pavement or swung around the lamp-posts till the rope tightened. Later, however, a whisper ran from Eccles Street, past Nelson Street, to Mountjoy Street by the Protestant School, the drab corner of Wellington Street, and St. Joseph's Convent: and I became aware obscurely of the new Edwardian age and the Life of Pleasure. For to live in sedate Eccles Street had come the Montagues, father and daughter. Mr. Montague was magnificent to see, for he always wore a frock coat and tall hat. Hilary Montague was tall, handsome, and red-haired, brilliant to watch in her three-quarter length coats of emerald and crimson, with large picture-hats to match. She was the only fashionable young woman in all the neighbourhood who used rouge and powder at a time when cheek-rubbing and eyebrow-wetting were signs of a doubtful reputation. Father and daughter were always setting forth to race meeting or theatre, or if not, were coming back from one or the other. Often we sped around a couple of corners on the chance of seeing them. Hilary Montague had a lot of men friends who were much younger than her father, and this occasioned much unworthy comment. Often we saw her being helped on to a side-car or off by an eager young man, escorted into or out of a cab.

We passed through Eccles Street on our way to St. George's Place, where our friends Mr. and Mrs. Storey had apartments in a house at the side of the Church. Built in the eighteenth-century classical style of white stone which took the soot gaily at its cornices, St. George's Church made me feel happy because it was so unlike the shadowy Victorian church at our corner. In the front parlour the aged mother of Mrs. Storey was always sitting in a much-worn armchair. Mrs. Hogarty's mind was dimming with age, like the minds of so many dear friends of mine nowadays, and as she nodded there, I suspect that but few flickerings of identity were left to her. On the other side of St. George's Church, I had had my own second flicker of self-identity when I was brought to the Children's Hospital with a threatened attack of meningitis at the age of three.

The horse-hair chairs in the parlour were pins-and-needles to my bare legs and meanly tormented me elsewhere for the short trousers which I wore in the summer were of calico. The windows were always tightly shut because Mrs. Hogarty was so old and there was a heavy odour in the parlour like stale snuff when all the tickles are gone. But the discomfort was well worth while. At the window was a large aquarium with several grotto arches though which goldfish swam. It had real pipes and a constant drip of water. I marvelled at that flow and whenever I bent over the glass tank, it was cold in that stuffy room, cold as the Vartry reservoir far away in Wicklow. Sometimes Mr. Storey, who was burly and red in the face, came in for his tea just as we were leaving. I was proud to know that man, for he was a Corporation solderer.

One day my mother brought her last two children to an unknown region beyond Lower Dorset Street. She was pushing the pram happily with Louis in it, not knowing that he, too, was to die so soon, and I was fribbing as usual with the tags of patent leather. We went along a wide pavement on which the shops bulged out with fruit stalls, furniture and hardware. We came at last to terraces of houses and street-trees, and as we perambulated under the wall of the ecclesiastical palace, beyond the high gates, I thought that the Archbishop of Dublin must be almost as great a personage as the Pope himself. Soon we were going down hill and when we reached the Tolka Bridge, we went by the side of it, to see on the river bank a little row of white-washed cottages, in front of which was a statue of the Blessed Virgin. My mother told me of the floods which were held back there by miraculous intervention. It was the first time, except in church grounds, that I had seen such a statue standing, all white and blue, in the open air.

Now that religion has come out of the churches to dwell amongst us, children have many more open-air statues to wonder at, particularly among the new building settlements, outside factories and transport firms. Dockers have drawn from their wage packets and we are to have a gigantic statue of the Virgin on the North Wall, illuminated at night, for the safe guidance of foreign ships. I confess that some of these new acts of devotion are not always quite edifying to people of old-fashioned belief. Often I pass, near Clanbrassil Street a small bulb-lit shrine of the Virgin in the window of a pork butcher's shop, glimmering feebly in the daylight, above chops, pig's feet, black and white puddings, legs of pork and boiled hams. A few yards away, near St. Nicholas Stores and St. Kevin's Stores are the drab Jewish shops with their kosher meats – so the Old Law and the New confront each other across the centuries. Trade now blesses itself for I have noticed, since Marian year, a number of new firms, such as Marian Office Equipment, Marian Printing Company, Marian Hats Manufacturers, Marian Clothing Company, Marian Fashions Ltd.: Mantles, Frocks, even Marian Saloon, Ladies' Hairdressers and Marian Hairdressing Saloons. In the country the devotion has gone apace and whenever I pass the Sancta Maria Poultry Farm in Co. Wicklow, called perhaps after the caravel of Columbus, I am tempted to think irreverently of that poem about St. Peter, written so long ago by W. B. Yeats when he was brooding over the 'Island of Statues'. Near Roscrea, as I stood before a holy statue outside the meat factory, I could hear, within, the click of the mercy-killer. Sometimes this new zeal has given way to a naughty temptation. At Kells, for example, the new statue of the Madonna is placed directly outside the Masonic Hall. But the apron-men have met, ladder-wise, that challenge to their second Commandment, for they have repainted boldly over the door-way the name of their building in Child of Mary blue.

The streets and laneway on the north side must have been very dingy, for I was astonished in childhood by the newness of the suburban avenues and groves on the south side of the city, all the more so because I was brought only on special occasions to those boroughs of delights – and spring seemed always there. The villas, with their brightly-painted hall-doors and lattices, were as gay as toys or picturebooks and around them all was a flower. On reading

De Profundis for the first time, I fancied that Oscar Wilde was writing of that lasting springtime:

> 'I tremble with pleasure when I think that on the very day of my leaving prison both the laburnum and lilac will be blooming in the gardens and that I shall see the wind stir into restless beauty the swaying gold of the one, and make the other toss the pale purple of its plumes so that all the air shall be Arabia to me.'

We passed those garden gates and gravel paths only when we were going to see Mrs. Annesley, who lived in the Magough Home for old Protestant ladies in reduced circumstances. On three sides of the quadrangle were the almshouses, each to itself, each on the right scale for the very young and the very old. Small as the houses were, the flowering shrubs seemed to hide from view even more delectable regions. Once, incautiously, I strayed under lilac and laburnum only to come on grief, for I found myself suddenly in a corner amid rubbish and saw below the wall a railway line and shabby backyards beyond it. I felt as if I had been transported by a djinn to the north side of Dublin. Mrs. Annesley had dwindled so daintily with age that she might have been thought of by Walter de la Mare. She gave me my first lesson in correct speech, and left me a joy which has increased with the years. It happened on an afternoon when I was to have, as a very special treat, a new-laid egg at afternoon tea.

'And how would you like it, my dear?'

'Rare, please.'

'Oh, you mean rear. 'Rare' is something unusual, something you don't see every day.' The old lady paused, as if she were trying to find among her whatnots some example for me.

I was so eager to show off that I nearly fell from the rocking chair.

'Would a ship on land be a rare sight, Mrs. Annesley?'

Many years later I discovered that the polite little lady was quite wrong. The older form of 'rear' is 'rare' and had probably remained in our local speech from Tudor times.

The new suburbs of Greater Dublin, so toylike, so English, with their tiny lawns and flowering shrubs, bring back to me again all that early delight. There is something toylike, too, in the frailty of those roomlets and kitchenettes, in which large adults have to move carefully as though they measured their movements by instalments. But the newness does not last very long after the concrete mixers have trundled out their slobs and slams for the blocking presses. The dashing dirties itself, the gates of unseasoned wood rot, cracks appear and, going by, I fancy sometimes that I can hear the plaster drop with minute oaths from the low ceilings.

Five

I

'WHAT time will you be back, Eileen?'

'We won't be later than seven o'clock, Mother.'

As my sister closed the hall door and glanced at the bright sky, we both felt very happy.

It was Holy Thursday and she was taking me with her to visit seven churches according to the pious custom which was peculiar to Dublin, but has recently been done away with by the ecclesiastical authorities. All the morning I had been looking forward with increasing excitement to that small pilgrimage of the city. We would have to be home at seven to give our mother an opportunity of visiting as many churches in the neighbourhood as she could, for my other sisters were away.

'I should have made out a list of churches,' said Eileen, 'to save time.'

As we went up Mountjoy Street, we decided not to visit St. Joseph's Convent because it was too near. We hurried past the barred windows of the Protestant school beyond the next corner, while I listened eagerly to her plans.

'First of all, we'll go to Berkeley Road Chapel. The short-cut through the grounds to the Mater only takes a minute, and Eccles Street Convent is a few doors away. That'll be three already. If we go down Eccles Street to Temple Street, we might, then, have time to run round to the Jesuits' in Gardiner Street, or better still, we could visit the Pro-Cathedral. It's not very far from Temple Street, and we could call in at Great Denmark Street Convent.'

'But couldn't we take a Whitehall tram?'

'No, we have to make the seven visits on foot. The Convent Chapel in Gloucester Street will probably be open to the public today.'

'And the Convent in Seville Place, near where Alice Synnot lives.'

'We could go back that way, or perhaps straight on to Clarendon Street. Yes, I think that'll be better.'

There was such a choice of churches and private chapels that it was hard to decide what to do.

'I should really have thought it all out this morning,' said my sister.

We had just turned the corner of Berkeley Road and gone past the shop which ten years later had political newspapers, illegal pamphlets and hurley-sticks in the window, when we saw Alice Connolly, Maura Deegan, Teresa Martin and Rose Murphy coming towards us. They were chatting happily together and must have just come from Berkeley Road Chapel. Eileen had completely forgotten that we might meet others making the same round, and I knew that she did not want to meet the girls, but they caught sight of us almost immediately and hurried forward with little greetings.

'Here's Eileen Clarke of all people, and Austin's with her!'

'We haven't seen you for a long time,' said Alice a little reproachfully.

'How many chapels have you done?' chimed in Teresa. 'This is our fourth.'

'I'm afraid we've only just started. Mother had to go out this morning.'

'We've been at it ever since half-two. We were thinking of going down to Dominick Street and then back to Phibsboro' and Aughrim Street.'

'Oh, Eileen, you should see Eccles Street. They've beautiful flowers and decorations this year – all white lilies. I simply loved it.'

'I was disappointed in William Street,' said Teresa. 'I think the altar was much nicer last year. Don't you, Rose?'

'I'm not so sure. I rather liked it, myself.'

'Why not come along with us?' said Alice.

'We're just going across to Berkeley Road for a minute.'

'Well, we'll come back with you,' laughed one of the girls. Eileen hesitated.

'We thought of going down town afterwards.'

'I know,' said Teresa, who was always a sly-boots, 'she doesn't want us with her.'

'I didn't mean that . . .'.

'I know what you mean,' said Rose in a kindly tone. 'You go along with Austin, and don't mind us.'

'Do you know, I'm dying for Easter Sunday. I hate giving up sweets for Lent,' confessed Maura.

'We know you do, but you make up for it on Sunday,' exclaimed Rose. 'It's just as well Sundays are not included.'

'I'm sure,' said Maura, looking at my sister quizzingly, 'you have some very special mortification.'

'Oh, we all know what Eileen has given up.' They had turned their heads from me.

'Well, remember us in your prayers.'

'Say a Hail Mary for me. It's for a very special intention,' murmured Rose, delaying for a moment after the others, and including me in that pious request with a smile.

Those happy voices sped around that corner. The tams, the tickly tresses, the jellybags and the woolly bobs were gone.

I knew of course that my sister no longer sat on the wall at the Broadstone corner near the gate lodge where the Gaynors lived, talking with girls and boys. She had changed very much since the year before, when she had been as care-free and light-hearted as her former companions and had made the seven visits with them. They had explored the south side of the city as far as Inchicore with its sacred grotto and the Crib which I was brought to see every Christmas. They had prayed in old and new churches that none of them had ever entered before. They met other bands of girls and compared likes and dislikes with them at the kerb, following up their joyful information. For on Holy Thursday the private chapels of convents, hospitals, colleges and institutions were open to the public. Always it was pleasant to come down from the richly laden, sumptuous oratory on the second floor, to smile at others on the crowded stair-case, to find and lose grown-ups in the coming and going, to hurry, talking through the busy streets, to meet family friends for a moment at the inner baize door of a church, or see them with bowed head, kneeling before the Blessed Sacrament. That day was, in a sense, the culmination of Lent and the exciting city pilgrimage in its alternation of daylight and candle-light had a festive, changing effect. In Lent itself was the same mixture of joy and novelty: the ashy cross which all received every Ash Wednesday on the forehead reminding them of their mortal end.

Sometimes the mark remained all day if the priest's thumb had been heavy, sometimes the blessed ashes were blown away by the morning air, frail as mortality. Even the fasting and minor mortifications were an adventure rather than a hardship. It was exciting to hurry home with the latest news from the altar.

'Owing to the severity of the winter, and the hardships of the poor, the fast will be relaxed.'

'Butter is allowed at two meals today, Mother.'

'We can have milk in our tea on Spy Wednesday.'

It seemed, indeed, as if by these special concessions, God was showing a paternal solicitude for weak mortals. There was a sense of gentleness and of kindliness that filled every soul with gratitude. In Lent, also, the Sundays were confectioned for, then, even our own private mortifications were suspended. The very palate was quickened in Lent by lesser excitements: the pancakes on Shrove Tuesday which opened the lenten season of seven weeks, colcannon taken with a wooden spoon from the pot on the range every fast-day, and on Good Friday the potted herrings with bayleaf and the Hot Cross Buns with their spices from the East. Holy Thursday, too, seemed all the brighter because at night the altar would be darkened under the black and purple pall. On Good Friday, in some churches, from noon, three hours were devoted to the Seven Last Words. In other churches the Stations of the Cross were recited and, as the congregation followed from aisle to aisle, from picture to picture, all seemed to be mingling with the multitude pressing through the narrow streets of Jerusalem, out to the rocks and open country, and then, as the great bells thumped out the third hour, the mourners moved to the altar steps to kiss the passing Crucifix.

A year or two before, on Easter Sunday, my sisters and I had crept to the top landing window at six o'clock to see beyond the cattle-sheds and the slates the sun dancing for joy. Only once, however, did we see that wonder.

Eileen had approached Lent gravely because of the change which had come over her during the last six months, though I was only dimly aware of that inner shining. She looked back with distress at the precious time she had wasted in foolish conversation and idle matters. She read holy books before she went to sleep at night, prized little leaflets for the indulgences they carried. She kept to herself that she might think of the acts of the saints, and walked with downcast eyes through the streets, avoiding the shop windows, fingering the rosary beads in her coat-pocket. The Nine Fridays had now a special significance for her. She undertook new novenas and when the Thirty Days' Prayer was over, she began it all over again. Every new aspiration, every indulgence of which she heard, whether attached to some special devotion or gained by visiting a shrine, whether symbolized by medal or scapular, drew her. I, too, had already felt the mysterious power of those scapulars which we wore, the brown scapular of St. Francis, the red, the white, the black one for the dead, the blue for the Blessed Virgin. So often the string broke and had to be knotted again, so soon the little holy picture printed on the white side became blurred from constant wear and perspiration. Some wore the scapular medal so as to avoid tape strings, for its use bore the same number of indulgences.

The very name indulgence had a strange ring: three hundred days of release from the pains of Purgatory, seven years remission from all that woe, and stranger still were the Plenary Indulgences, one of which could send the soul straight up into the glory of heaven. To handle those medals, or those pink leaflets, was to know that a few words truly repeated could, if we went on adding one to another, save us from the flame and torture which we all deserved.

Half a minute after we had left Alice Connolly, Maura Deegan, Teresa Martin and Rose Murphy, we were at Berkeley Road Church, the cold touch of marble on our wet finger tips, as we made the sign of the Cross and came towards the sanctuary. The nave, which was empty and dark, brought to our minds the next day. The High Altar was hidden in a black and purple pall, and although I knew that I should not genuflect before it, I went past the nave with some apprehension. Even the small gilt door of the tabernacle was draped in mourning. Not until the morrow, at the solitary Mass of the Presanctified, would an already consecrated Host be brought processionally from a side-altar. Often my sisters and I had knelt at the end of the nave on quiet winter evenings when only the wine-red glow of the sanctuary lamp made the suspensory chains glitter and the tabernacle, half-seen between its diminutive curtains, caught the last faint light of day. We loved that silence, disturbed only by the noise of a passing tram outside, or the footsteps of a few sinners coming in to pray.

Beyond the pillars, we could see the glitter of the tapers on a side-altar and we made our way, softly, towards the small crowd kneeling before the brass triangles of light, with their slowly dropping wax. My sister bowed her head as if she were at the Forty Hours Exposition and I copied her very carefully. The stillness of the Exposition had always filled me with mingling awe and uneasiness. For something always tempted me, trying to make me look up at the paleness glassed in the gold monstrance. In a puzzling way, I felt that there was some irreverence in that ceremony for at Mass the presence of the priest in his alb and chasuble seemed to come between the soul and the visible mystery. When the altar boy sounded the gong before the Elevation, it was a sign for all to bow their heads. At Benediction, also, as soon as the officiant had mounted the step-ladder and placed the monstrance in the niche, the floating clouds of frankincense from the thurible almost concealed the oriflamme. When he took down the monstrance again, and, wrapping its base in the folds of the humeral veil, blessed us, we did not dare to look up.

We knelt for a little while at the end of a bench, moving back at times to let others come or go. Then we left by a side-door. The iron gate which led to the church grounds was open, and we passed the rockeries and the shrubs. We decided not to go to the Mater Hospital, and in a moment or two found ourselves outside the area railings of Eccles Street Convent.

The staircase, with its deep carpeting which hushed every foot-fall, was crowded and we had to wait with others on the landing before entering the small chapel. People lowered their voices as if they were aware of their intrusion, although on a public day such as this the community remained out of sight. As we passed the large black screen at the oratory door, a sudden sweetness came to us: the strange entranced perfume of the lilies in rigid rows, the faint mingling odours from masses of white hot-house flowers. Through these came a stab of acrid fume from a candle that had burned awry, been extinguished and silently replaced. In that tense place there was scarcely way for our knees or elbows, yet we felt both the intimacy and aloofness. Before the altar, two nuns were kneeling on prie-dieux, white-hooded, completely motionless. I knew instinctively that tension of private and public devotion, in which each is aware of others, for too often I had felt what all children enjoy, the guilty pleasure of being very good. The statue-like stillness of those white figures, the minute restlessness and glittering of the candles, the getting up and down, the coming-and-going, the unearthly hush were strange yet familiar to me. My sister seemed to have forgotten the time as she knelt there with flushed cheek. I plucked at her sleeve and we made our way down quietly past the throng to meet the cold air outside.

We passed the Temple Street convent in our haste and were about to retrace our steps when we saw two girls whom we knew, so instead we decided to go to the city churches. We hurried down Great Denmark Street hill and, almost as if we had been transported by angels, found ourselves on the broad steps of the Pro-Cathedral. That large church was different from all the others for it was possible to tip-toe along the ambulatory, past the pillars, the flowers and king-candles to see the back of the High Altar which was always a surprise to me because it was so blank and drab. The semi-circles of candles in the Chapel of Repose on that Holy Thursday seemed mere twinkles until we came towards them. There was a large crowd and we only stayed a moment, for beyond the lessening bridges of the Liffey were parish churches, darker and more mysterious, their altar-joys summoning us. . . .

II

We always found it exciting to leave the crowded pavement of Grafton Street, turn the corner, find ourselves in the narrow alley outside the gate of Clarendon Street Church. But on this occasion, Johnson's Court was full of people who were making their seven visits. We had just come out of the church when, to our consternation, we banged right into our friends, Alice Connolly, Maura Deegan, Teresa Martin and Rose Murphy.

'Why, here we all are again!'

'How many chapels have you done, Eileen?'

'Three . . . I mean. . .'

'Four,' I hastened to add.

'We did our seven, so we took a number eleven tram down town and thought we'd look in here, for a change.'

We escaped from them at last and went by the covered archway of the south City Market, with its fruit and fish stalls, into George's

Street. We were safe from those teasers and I hugged my sister's arm as we went along for I knew of course that Thomas à Kempis had written of those small daily trials which we must learn to endure. As we walked up Aungier Street we were aware of the communion of the saints, the communion of the living and the dead: the hosts in Heaven; the people passing by the lamp-posts; the furniture stores and ironmongery shops and the hidden millions in Purgatory. The Church Triumphant in Heaven, the Church Suffering in Purgatory, the Church Militant on Earth: the phrases rang with magnificence, though the pride and historic anger were beyond my comprehension. The sun was hotter in the sky, for we were no longer coming towards Camden Street, but were on the Continent. We were in the streets of Padua where St. Anthony had prayed, in the narrow byways of Dijon where Francis de Sales met Madame de Chalmey, at Charolles where Blessed Margaret Mary had her visions. The Sacrament was being borne by angels through the clouds to dying lips far below: the sick were on stretchers outside holy grottoes; we were in the fever- stricken thoroughfares of Rome in a remote century. Suddenly we were back in Dublin, crossing the road to the church at Whitefriar Street corner. The large crucifix within the porch was partly hidden by a triangular pall that pointed downwards: it looked queer that way as if it had been put on upside down. As we came in, the figures in the stained glass were calm, their leaded outlines dark against the last evening light.

By turnings and side-streets, past Bull Alley and Engine Row, we came to Francis Street Church. We thought of going over to Meath Street, but the Augustinian Church was nearer so we chose it. We delayed some time there for we went over to the opposite aisle after we had left the altar, because the shrine of St. Anne looked so lonely. There were only a few candles guttering on the brass frame in front of it, so I dropped a penny in the box, lit a candle for both of us and placed it on one of the eleven empty spikes. When we came out, the sky was overcast and we knew we must hurry. Soon those who were at work all day would be coming to make their seven visits. We wondered whether we would have time to say a few prayers at St. Audeon's. We loved those older churches, their walls so high above the shabby streets, the gas-lit, sawdusted shops of the Liberties. They were so shadowy, their bench-steps worn by congregations long since forgotten.

As our pilgrimage was over, we could wait for the Ballybough tram at the corner of Capel Street Bridge, and take a penny ticket to Rutland Square. We walked along Winetavern Street, trying to remember all the other churches which we could have visited. When we left Clarendon Street, we could have gone up to Cardinal Newman's chapel in Stephen's Green, passed by the large house where a miraculous cross has been seen in a top window, gone into the Loreto Convent and St. Vincent's Hospital, then visited the Marist Fathers just around the corner of Leeson Street, and immediately opposite the Convent of the Sacred Heart. We might have gone to Baggot Street Convent, Haddington Road Church and the Convent of the Holy Faith near it, back to St. Andrew's at Westland Row and . . . and . . . It was difficult to remember the saintly names of parish churches, and chapels belonging to religious orders: The Carmelites, the Discalced Carmelites, the Augustinians, the Franciscans, the Dominicans near our home, the Passionists at Mount Argus, the Fathers of the Holy Ghost, the Marists, Jesuits, Redemptorists, Vincentians, all those names excited us by their foreign sound. There were so many churches in the city that it would take us days and days to visit them all, although most of them were only a few streets away from each other – and there would be more, after that, in the faraway suburbs.

Halfway across Winetavern Street, we could see against the dark clouds not only the distilleries and brewery, but the high spire of St. Augustine's in Thomas Street which we had just visited. A few people were going into the Franciscan Church on the Quay. It would only take us a minute and I wanted to see the candelabra and the flowers at Adam and Eve's. So we went back across the bridge and made our eighth visit.

When we came out, a few raindrops were falling, and we hurried past the balustrades of the bridge.

'I wish we had time to go to Merchant's Quay Chapel or over to Ussher Quay.'

'And Halston Street beyond the Four Courts. It's only a few steps from there to the Franciscans in Church Street.'

At that moment the Ballybough tram came.

Six

I

THERE were several aspidistras in our parlour window, the pots hidden in a black stand, and through the few inches left a small boy could press close to the pane. As often as not another small boy and his brother appeared beside the aspidistras in the parlour window of the larger house immediately opposite ours. It was some years before I met those other starers, though our glances seemed to meet across the road as we watched dray or watering-cart go by. The household over there concealed some mystery of its own, for the older members of it were men and women, while the younger were boys and girls. The mother of them all was a dumpy, grey-haired woman and her husband was grey-whiskered, bald. The double name of the family, O'Brien and Moriarty, puzzled me and in a vague way I felt that there must be something wrong about second marriages, although I had not heard as yet of my grandfather's fall from grace.

The main event every day in our street occurred at half past five in the evening, when, in rapid succession, cabs and outside cars came up St. Mary's Place, around the far side of the Black Church, on the way to meet the Galway train. They raced past the open gates of the private road, opposite the Church, which led to the Broadstone Station. Not long afterwards, they swept back again, with clatter, jingle and rattle of harness, past our side of St. Mary's Place. Although most of them had travellers, a cab or outside car, sometimes, came back empty, but always the horse held its head up bravely. Often I ran to the window or even to the gate of our little garden outside with its dusty shrubs, to see Uncle John, Cab and Car Proprietor, in elegant tweeds, drive by on his outside car, coaxing his favourite brown mare. I watched him come, with expert flick of whip, looking straight ahead and yet talking over his shoulder to tourist or stranger up from the country. As he entertained his fare, I seemed to hear the American twang in his voice which always sounded so sarcastic to me. I felt very proud of him, for I knew he was a great jarvey.

So, swiftly and eagerly, those drivers went by every evening in the week, still undeterred by a century of steam. On wet days they were wrapped in heavy overcoats or oilskins, and on winter evenings, the brass and silver lamps, with their tallows in long sockets, threw a faint glow. But another age was coming and, unwittingly, I had a glimpse of it one day when my father brought me on the handlebars of his bicycle to Park Gate Street. In a dizzying whirl of noise, fire and fume, the Gordon-Bennett racing cars leaped past on their way to the Phoenix Monument. They were as monstrous as the machines which schoolboys read about a few years later in their comic papers, when with eyes over-full of serial pictures, they turned to the stories in small print to make up more exciting pictures with the inner eye.

Earlier in the afternoon the Black Maria came up Dominick Street, past the tenements and the huxter shops at the corner. As it went by, we could see the faces of men and women, their hands clutching the bars of the high narrow window at the back of the van. They shouted, sang, laughed or were sullen, and we stared without much thought at those creatures who belonged to what were known as the lower orders, in those days of stern British rule. The Black Maria went on its way, past Blessington Street and the Mater Misericordiae Hospital, to Mountjoy prison, with its grey stone walls beside the Royal Canal locks.

The horses that lumbered with the prison van are gone, but little has changed in our Ill-fare State. In one of his poems, Thomas Kettle spoke of the 'secret scripture of the poor', a phrase which has puzzled the pious. Once on the wall of an old estate above the common opposite the Loughlinstown workhouse, in County Dublin, I saw, during an election campaign, a sentence painted in large white letters, which might have been taken from that unwritten testament: 'The Poor Have no Friends. They Have Only Their Rights.' But Heaven alone knows what those rights are. Today the children of the poor suffer in increasing numbers the fate of their unworthy parents, for when they err, they are imprisoned in houses of correction, in charge of religious orders.

One afternoon at four o'clock, a cab came slowly around the

corner of the Broadstone Road and drove up our street. There was a hush and all the lace curtains stirred. Clearly through the cab window we could see the grey face of a bulky man, known as the Mullingar Murderer. He had strangled a girl forty miles away on the bank of the Royal Canal, and in a few weeks, he, too, would die, by strangulation, beside the same canal.

Two hours after that cab had passed at its funeral pace, we heard the customary rattle, jingle and tattle of harness as the drivers came around St. Mary's Place, vying with one another, on their way to meet the express from Galway. All is changed now for those nervous, intelligent animals, so quick to reins, are bred for export because of the appetite of Continental horse-eaters. But to spare such animals the sufferings of a sea-voyage, we are to set up in a short while a slaughter-house in our capital to prove our kindness and increase our profits, having as our motto: Straight from Stable to Table.

Often Aunt Ciss called for us with her pony and trap to take us on drives to the nearby countryside. Certainly we visited the Strawberry Beds, sloping towards the Liffey below Knockmaroon Hill, with their tea-cottages and taverns. We must have been at Celbridge, at the Waxies Glen, and once we were at Lucan Looks Lovely. At the Spa there, I gulped a glassful of the famous dirty water. It cost only a couple of pence and yet it tasted as if a shilling's worth of coppers had been dissolved in it with their tiny Queen Victoria heads, Britannias, shields and all. We were at Glendalough, too, on a Sunday. There was a big hotel near a waterfall hidden behind trees and on the level ground between the two lakes were crowds of merry-makers. A few Sundays later, my sister Kathleen was brought on a pleasure-ship which went around Dublin Bay and cried to be taken off 'the floating public house'.

I have forgotten much of what I saw on those trips, for I was always facing the large, wagging hinderparts of the pony and was surprised on each occasion by that sudden change from the spiritual refinement of our home life. I must have endured much, so constantly were three of my senses offended. I knew that acts of natural necessity are permitted to us all if we do not take pleasure in them and that animals cannot sin because they have no souls. Nevertheless I shrank back whenever modesty was offended. Was there a false ring in our voices when we raised them so as not to hear what the pony was doing? Was our sudden interest in the hedgerows and fields we passed too obvious? It was all very puzzling to me, for the pony was an intelligent animal, in front, with demure glance; and his grey-black mouth was affectionate though somewhat fumbling to a small palm. All the more did I enjoy our return journey through darkness, when his base rounds were hidden and I was warm among rugs, drowsing in the well of the trap.

Quite often we drove to the Featherbed Mountain above Dublin, so called from the bogcotton which grows abundantly there, and near Glencree, we picked fraughans or whortleberries for the delicious pies which Aunt Ciss made. We had tea and home-made bread in a cottage which was the only one above the glen. It was owned by an elderly couple, Mr. and Mrs. Dunne, but I did not know at the time that Mrs. Dunne was a wise woman who gathered medicinal herbs on the mountain side. The room off the kitchen, where we sat at our meal, had a large window and a wonderful press with a bed concealed in it. From the ridge outside, we could see the wicked boys working in the fields of the Reformatory below, or marching up and down its prison yard with a Black Brother as their grim jailer. Years afterwards, the couple seemed no older, when I used to stay in the cottage for brief holidays and sleep in that press-bed. Frequently at morning, youths are rigid when they wake up, so potent is the Devil, and our confessors bid them be on their guard. Only when I went to England did I learn from a sensible writer that this diabolical manifestation, which had caused me so much spiritual anxiety, was really due to the pressure of urine. So, fearing the Adversary, I always jumped up early, ran through the heather, stripped again in guilty haste and swam about the small reservoir which supplied water to the boy-prisoners and the terrible Black Brethren in the great building below.

Eventually the two old people died, and the empty cottage sank almost as quickly as they into the earth from which it had been raised.

After a time my aunt refused to take me for any more drives because I asked too many questions, yet I like to think that my tongue-wagging may have been due partly to embarrassment whenever the pony lifted its tail. I remember clearly our last evening on the Featherbed Mountain because of a moment of alarm, when my cousin Johnnie induced me to run down to a hollow, remained at the top and threw stones at me as I cowered there: a moment of grief, when we found in a narrow boreen between loose stone walls a yellowhammer on the ground, the brightest bird I had as yet seen, quite still after its last little flutter: a moment of terror, when I saw for the first time a mountain tarn. The terror happened at darkfall, after we passed the cottage in which J. M. Synge might have been staying at the time. We rounded a corner and between rocks, I saw suddenly the cold gleam of Lough Bray. Overcome by some elemental dread, I caught the hand nearest to me and turned away.

My first holiday in the country was when my sister, Doto and I went to stay with family friends, Mary Nixon and her mother, at Valleymount in County Wicklow. Miss Nixon, who was the schoolteacher there, lived in the cottage beside the church. Despite this fact, I found myself, without guidance, in a region that seemed to me beyond the catechism.

II

It was darkfall as we hurried past the terrible, shadowy trees and came to the wicket. All might have happened in a story, for the diamond panes of the cottage, beside the church, were merry with lamplight. But there were tiny paths, edged with box in the little garden, which I had to explore before they disappeared completely. I can still remember those scarlet and white flowers shaped like stars which I saw there for the first time and can remember their perfume. The night was coming faster; voices were mingling at the cottage door, and I knew that I had only a few minutes to see all these strange flowers. Then, in some confused way, I met Theresa in that dimming garden. I wanted to stay and look at the starry flowers. But that little girl, with a toss of her ringlets, and with the authority of one who had already been a month in the country, led me down the small winding paths to a yard gate.

'I want to show you something,' she said in a mysterious tone, and I obeyed her implicitly.

So while our elders were still talking on the door step, she led me across the cobbled yard to a shed.

'Look!' she said. 'Look!'

I cannot remember seeing anything at all, but she was pointing into the darkness of the shed, and certainly, I must have obeyed her and leaned through the doorway in great curiosity. But soon the call of voices startled us.

'Theresa! Theresa! . . . Where on earth are those children?'

We hastened in without a word.

The next morning, much to my astonishment, there was a strange air of severity above our small heads, a foreboding silence in the cottage, which dashed all those feelings of joy I should have felt on my first morning in the country. Something terrible had happened the night before. A broody hen had been frightened off its clutch by one or other of us. We were both summoned to judgment. The very charge was inexplicable to me and I was unable to understand: all I knew was that something very dreadful had happened and that I was innocent. Even grown-ups can prove poor witnesses under cross examination, and I was oppressed by that sense of injustice which all children feel so acutely.

'He did it!'

I can still remember my astonishment and confusion when that little girl, shaking her curls, pointed an accusing finger at me and blandly told how I had led her astray.

The country itself was even more deceptive than that small Eve whom I met in the garden where the flowers only came out at twilight. A furze bush, the twisted wires of a fence, the green marshy grass in the corner of the small fields were all capable of sudden and unexpected treachery. At home I knew every corner of the small backyard and garden. The centre path was the main track for express trains, the rockery in the far corner was Port Arthur, for ever defended by the Russians, for ever stormed and almost taken in assault by the Japanese. If I kept to the pavement, when I went for messages down Capel Street, and hurried past the children who were playing their part also in the Russo-Japanese war, if in fact I obeyed the common-sense rules of travelling, I was quite safe. But in the country the fields and turf banks were strange and unmapped. Nothing was what it seemed and everything was something else. The furze bushes waited until we were almost past and then struck at us viciously, the fencing-wire lay in ambush to tear our clothes, the grass tumbled us into depths of mud. Joys and tears were never so close and we were always falling into mischief and out of mischief. Those fairy tales which Eileen read out to me sometimes or told me when we were walking past the sweetshops in Capel Street all seemed to be true. Nothing was quite what it seemed and if one lit on fairy gold, it would almost certainly turn into a handful of withered leaves. There was an animus in nature against which I had to struggle, for Dublin was far away and I was evidently in a region beyond the strict guidance of the catechism.

Now that the reservoir dam at Poulaphouca has been completed, flood is rising to the last ridge below Valleymount and another sky has tumbled into the heather. The narrow lands, from which my father's people came, have vanished under water and the trout are too heavy to jump. But in those far-off days when I first saw Valleymount, there was one sunny height where we were all safe from the animus of nature. We could roll happily down the slope of polished grass or pull to our hearts' content the tiny golden trefoil. It was exciting to nip those lucky three-leaves almost at the root and weave them into bracelets and many loops. We were safe, and yet not entirely so, for there was a mystery among the mountains at Wicklow Gap.

Whenever we looked south we could see the small farmhouse at the top of the last hill below the mountains. An old woman of fabulous age lived there, and my eldest sister had brought us to see her early one evening. As we came to the farmhouse we passed into an immense sunny stillness. No dogs barked and along the wall of the cobbled yard the hens were drowsing and scarcely lifted a grey eyelid as we went by. There was a well-head in the middle of the yard with a rusty chain and we were afraid to look down into the horrible depth below. We stole to the open door and peeped in. A clock was ticking loudly in the silent kitchen; we saw a drawn curtain and knew that the centenarian must be asleep. So we never met her, but often after that, as we played on the sunny slope, we were aware of that distant farmhouse on the hill-top and it disturbed us vaguely like a legend. There is indeed something legendary in that terrible waiting of the aged as the human faculties slowly decay until memory itself persists only in the sharp anguish of dream; and who can name that minute before dawn when such poor creatures of a century waken and believe that they are long since dead? When, in later years, I came on the story of the Old Woman of Beare, the great Knee-woman of Ireland, and other mysthic personages, I thought always of that silent farm-yard, over which the sun had stopped, and of the hens drowsing outside the empty stable, lazily blinking a grey eyelid.

On the evening before we left Valleymount the animus of nature suddenly increased. It happened that I was taken for a walk by my elders. We went along the sandy shore, the green-edged creeks of the King's River, and as it was the first time that I had been near the lonely winding river, I had brought with me for this special trip a glass jar complete with the inevitable string. It was a long journey and, as my elders walked through the twilight, we passed marvellous pools along the edge of the river strand, full of darting minnow. I wanted to linger at these pools and catch some of the minnow, but those elders hurried on and every time I hesitated with my glass jar at some pool, they called to me to come along. Darkness was setting in as we started back on our homeward journey along the river sands. The pools were still glimmering, but I could no longer find again those in which I had seen so many pinkeens – and then I came to a pool which I seemed to remember. This was my last chance and, though I was afraid of remaining behind even for a few moments in the half light, I took the risk. In the dimness I saw that the pool was full of little fish and I dipped in the jar. The water rushed in with a satisfying gurgle, and as I lifted up the jar again, I could see even in the darkness that it was full of minnow.

I could scarcely wait until we had got back to the cottage again. As soon as we were inside, I ensconced myself in my favourite place, beside the harmonium: I held up the glass jar in the lamplight. I looked into a small mysterious green world: But instead of those lovely minnow I saw a sight which filled me with horror. The minnow had been changed mysteriously into little monsters which were magnified by the thick glass. Were they specimens, as the learned might say, of hydrobatidae or rhynchota? It did not occur to me that these struggling forms were a few half-drowned water-skaters and spiders which had been engulfed in the glass jar. I only felt that here once more was the treachery of nature and that in the country nothing is what it seems and everything is something else.

But my last experience of the country on that first visit was yet stranger. Farewells were over; the pony and trap had gone; and we were waiting at Featherbed Lane for the steam-tram from Poulaphouca. It was almost night but, greatly daring, I strayed back around the corner of the lane. Suddenly I stopped in superstitious dread; for there, black and horned against the last light of the west on the lofty bank above the laneway, was a motionless god-like image. By some obscure intuition I recognized the awful mithraic form. The ancient myths still linger even in the Liberties of many a city: and my father had told me so often at night the story of the Brown Bull and of the Horn of Plenty, had told it to me so patiently, each time, that I knew it by heart and in my sleep. The Bull in that vestigial story was benevolent despite its supernatural strength. But this black image against the sky never moved in its terrible watchfulness. Such seconds of fear become as valuable to us as years. But for those seconds I do not think that I would have glimpsed that ancient piety and awe hidden in the cattle stories of Connaught and Ulster, the great Táin Bo Cuailgne.

I was back again with my elders by the track; and soon the steam-tram, with its cheerful infernal noise and brimstone, was rushing past suddenly-seen hedges towards us. In its noise and smut we were swept back to the city and the catechism.

III

Often as I watched the four-wheelers and the two-wheelers, with their eager drivers, coming around St. Mary's Place, past the Black Church, on their way to the terminus, I longed to travel into the country in one of the Great Western trains. The day came at last when Ned Marmion, a family friend, took me for a holiday to his sister's cottage in County Meath near the River Boyne. Much to my surprise, on our arrival at Kilmessan, we did not leave the station with the other few passengers, but went down the platform, out by a wicket gate, and across fields heavy with June. After a quarter of an hour we came to the cottage and while his sister, Mary, was getting the tea ready, Ned took me down the road towards the river. We stopped at a gate-post and I saw, for the first time, hundreds of rabbits gambolling and feeding in a large, hillocky field, a sight which children in the future may never enjoy. We ventured along the avenue of an old estate, and in the grass beside it, plucked wild strawberries to bring back with us. They were so minute that I was disappointed with them, being used to the large ones we bought in town. But they were a delight to the poet, F. R. Higgins, who spent much of his childhood in County Meath about this time and used to pick them at Balivor, for he has written a lyic about them which will be found in his first book of verse.

It was in Meath that I made my first acquaintance with the Devil. I had scarcely attained to that age of reason which comes in normal cases, according to some theologians, about the seventh winter of life, and being as yet incapable of mortal sin, I was beyond the reach of the medieval fork. I could afford, therefore, to observe the sinister activities of that spirit with curiosity rather than with fear. On many nights in the small cottage – hidden in a rustling corner of that lost province to which I can only find the road back with difficulty – as we sat around the turf fire on the open hearth, and as I bent towards sleep, a horseshoe, a bolt, or some other unbreakable object, that had been shaped in a hotter place, fell, with a loud clatter, down the chimney.

'There's the Old Boy again,' the neighbours, who had come in for a talk, were accustomed to exclaim, as they examined the latest specimen of materialization or ectoplasmic metal with serious interest and wonder. On the final night of these manifestations – more suitable, I have since thought, to a poltergeist or playful elemental than to the Spirit of Evil – a curious object of wrought iron rattled, with a certain cheerful familiarity, at my feet. Now, it so happened that I had been, in secret, troubled by the nature of a similar object which hung upon the whitewashed wall and which, on grown reflection, I fancy to have been only a stand for a smoothing-iron. Looking, then, towards the wall, I saw that the nail was empty and at the same time I heard someone clambering down from the low thatched roof outside. The arithmetical conclusion was simple, but my suspicions were laughed at rather than allayed, and on that night the chance seed of a later scepticism may have been dropped carelessly and the Devil, after all, have had his due.

'The lads come here to play pitch and toss on wet days,' said the tall man; who was my companion, when we came for the first time under the railway bridge. Soon afterwards he took to himself a drapery shop and a wife in the small town near the ruined Castle of King John, and a few years later, I heard that he was dead.

'They lose their pennies,' he said, that day long ago, 'in the grass.'

We searched and found several of the lost pence; and after that, our steps always led us along the quiet road to the railway bridge. Yet, despite my scrupulous endeavours, I could never find more than the two or three coppers which were sufficient to provide less sweets than could make a small boy ill. Upon a wettish day, that vanished man picked up a silver coin from a spot which I had just left. As I had searched behind every blade of grass there, my mind was stirred by sudden suspicions. Yet I am still forced to believe in those invisible young fellows who wagered head and harp upon that road, and sometimes, on a rainy Sunday evening, I can hear the chink of coins before they fall into nothing. We are bred among stories that are older than ourselves and we disappear from sight, with the last-aid of a little Latin, in the fond hope that all cannot be rot.

Of the older boy who stayed in the large white farmhouse behind the opposite gate, I remember little – only the moral fact that he was very bold. On a quiet sunny afternoon, when hens were tired and there was no sound but that of a far drowsy scythe, we stole into the abandoned kitchen where the fire was asleep and milk pans were bright along the wall. We climbed the rickety ladder to the loft, for despite every warning, we forgot that an aged ghost lived there. Beneath the dark rafters, terror stirred and assailed me, and him, no doubt, for with a simultaneous shriek, we hurried down the shaky rungs of that ladder, and did not cease our outcry until we sat, trembling, on a distant gate.

Fear leaps to blinding consciousness in a child, but conceals itself from new sight or sound. So we hurried, soon, to the pigsty, and with that astounding cruelty of the young, their spiteful sense of injurious fate, armed with switches, one standing at the door, one within, we harried the unfortunate groundlings. With shame and redness of cheek, I have remembered how those pigs raced in a frantic circle; have heard the ceaseless roundabout of screeches that would have appeased the little ear of Circe. I can but hope now that our infant arms were less powerful than the din around us. Pleasantly we think that children see with the sidelong clarity of a young bird, or of a rabbit who has come up for the first time, to moist grass, but if we are honest with ourselves what is left of all our looking? Meath is no longer a province and so it was in the rustling corner of a lost province that I first heard of Tara and knew that the name contained mysteries. Yet I have forgotten the actual moment when I stood at nightfall on that royal hill, knowing nothing of the invisible centuries around me and all their furious imagining. I can only remember that a sad woman brought me there through the twilight, along low ridges, and past many thorn-trees, and that her voice was soft as milk. She told me that there had been a great battle near the Boyne long ago and that the shamrocks were still stained with the blood of the poor croppies. We picked several of these brown-stained shamrocks on the very edge of night, but when I came back years after, I could not find them any more.

Seven

ALTHOUGH water has always been a religious symbol, daily little acts of devotion tend to deprive the element of its mysteriousness. As often as not, when I dipped my fingers into the font at the church porch and made the Sign of the Cross, I did so off-handedly and from sheer habit. I was always aware indeed of the chill touch of the marble rim and occasionally when the holy water had not been changed for some time, the grit left by so many hands disturbed me and I felt vaguely that it should not be there. At home, all was different. I had an unfailing reverence for common water, because we were told that not a drop of it must be wasted. This family lesson was due to the fact that my father was Superintendent of the Dublin Waste Water Department. Whenever there was a drip from the scullery tap, he hastened to replace the washer; and a burst pipe in winter was never an occasion for alarm and sudden helplessness. For me, indeed, it was an occasion of joy. My father, who was a self-made man, had never forgotten his early years and he took his implements eagerly from the cupboard under the stairs. First of all was the spirit lamp, the very name of which seemed to have a religious significance, and I listened in awe to the dull roar of the flame, a little fearful lest the lamp should explode. Then came the soldering iron, which silvered, crisped, flaked, when it was dipped into the dumpy metal pot, and lastly the thick cloth pad, blackened and greasy, for wiping the new, gleaming joint. I watched my father at work, taking a solemn pleasure in his skill and certainty of touch. To add to all this pride of mine – we had a water-key of our own and could turn off the supply from the main in the street outside. Moreover everybody knew that my father had an instinctive knowledge of his own although he had never passed any examination. Whenever the water inspectors had failed to locate a leak in house or under roadway, he came, listened and found the exact spot, for he knew every wile and sound of water. Always he carried in his pocket a small wooden stethoscope. Nowadays, water-inspectors use a rubber roller, with an electric battery and ear-phones, but this new instrument is not always a match in cunning for a hidden lead pipe laid almost a century ago.

We could see the Dublin Mountains from some of the higher streets; and beyond them, far away in Wicklow, was the reservoir at Roundwood. I longed to go there, because my father had told me often of the mysterious blue clay which kept the waters from disappearing. I was aware always of the reservoir, for in summer when there was a danger of drought, my father grew anxious, as inch by inch the level of the water dropped and he scanned the daily reports in his office, but all was well again when the inevitable rains broke. It was a joy to think that, inch by inch, the reservoir was rising, the numerals on the gauges steadily mounting. In winter, when the torrential rain doubled along the pavements or caught umbrellas in gusts at the corner of the Black Church, I knew that there would be mighty supplies for the city. As the rain beat against the windows, I delighted in the noise of the gutters and drains. I could turn on a tap without too much care, pull the chain in the bathroom at the top of the house, or dashing through downpour, flush the water-closet in the backyard, next to the coal-shed, without straining my conscience.

At last came the summer day when my sisters and I set out for our holidays at Vartry Lodge, Roundwood. Beyond the sudden clatter of the long and short tunnels at Bray, the train hurried onward, stopped at a small, lonely station on the coast. Mr. Farrell, the caretaker, was waiting for us with his trap.

We drove from the sea, along a road across the brown saltings and came to a very steep hill. Slowly we reached the top and saw among trees a Valve House: the huge mains were silent, yet I knew that the water was rushing through them down to the city and to our own scullery tap. The road twisted among the heatherlands and at last, turning a corner on the left, we saw suddenly between woods of fir, the lake which hundreds of men had made. In a minute or two, we were at the gates of Vartry Lodge and atop of the piers were metal sea-horses like those on Capel Street Bridge. At the end of the short gravel drive, beyond laurels, was the Lodge itself and I knew at a glance that it was a place of enchantment, for it was like a chateau in a fairy tale, with square tower and peaked roof of blue slate. To complete the joy, the tower had a lightning conductor, just like the one on the spire of the Black Church, but much nearer and therefore easier to examine. Only too soon, however, I found that the Lodge also had its forbidden rooms into which we dare not tiptoe. These rooms on the west side had wonderful french windows which opened on to a terraced lawn, but they were reserved for Mr. Eyre, the City Engineer and other great officials. We were to stay with the caretaker and his family in the back of the house and, as at home, have our meals in the kitchen.

The Farrell children took instant possession of me for I was of their own age and all of them wanted to show me everything at once. Down the gravel drive again, past the laurels and the sea-horses, we darted across the road to the low wall of the reservoir. A short iron bridge led out to the water tower but its high gate was locked. The lake seemed so long that I could hardly see the far end of it; on each side the woods came down to the stony shores. Soon we were back at the little avenue for I had to be shown the filter beds without any further delay. There was a path almost hidden by laurels just inside the gate and we hurried along it; between the fir trees on our left I could see meadow grass, and on our right was the ever-deepening slope of the embankment with its great granite sets. Never before had I stumbled on the long roots of trees and at every step the gnarled path became more uneven. Suddenly one of the youngsters darted into the grass between the trees and searched around while I waited in joyful expectation, for the others told me that they had found a wild bees' nest there the day before and some of the honey might be left in it. Jack shouted as he found it again. I was given a bit of the comb but, as I crunched it, the sweetness changed to a horrible grey taste and I spat the cells out into my hand. They were filled with queer little grubs. I remembered what had happened to me at Valleymount and it seemed to me that once more the animus of nature was working and nothing was what it seemed. The children laughed and in a moment I had forgotten that shock and yet it remained – for the taste has never left my mouth.

We came to the last turning of the path and went down some steps and I saw the filter beds, oblong after oblong, their waters calm and shining in the evening light. Nearby in a grove of laurels was a bust on a pedestal which resembled the Roman Emperors in one of my schoolbooks, though it must have been only that of the engineer who had planned the reservoir. There was an arched tunnel under the embankment and I peered through the railings at strange wheels and levers, listening in some anxiety to the rumble of hidden waters. I was glad when we left the grove and ran over to an immense ornamental basin, in the middle of which five or six fountain jets were playing. As we darted around it, the spray, half circling with the light breeze, tried to reach us.

It might have been all a fairy tale for that night my happiness disappeared. As soon as I had said my prayers and got into bed, the unfamiliar room, the dark branches which I could see outside the window against the moonlight, the silence, so strange to a city child, filled me with uneasiness, although I was not alone for Kathleen was in the other bed in the far corner. After a while, I noticed that the moonlight shining on the counterpane was unusually bright and I remembered that moment of dread when I had seen the water-gleam among the rocks above Glencree. I closed my eyes but I could not escape from the strange moonlight. It was all around me even when I hid my head under the bed-clothes. I seemed to be both in the room and at the same time outside under the sky. The moon was shining on the wide waters all around the house and making them as bright as itself. Without a sound, the level of the lake was rising and the numerals on the gauges were being covered. I closed my eyes again but I could not find darkness. There was nothing now but that flood-gleam and when I opened my eyes, they might have been closed for the flood-gleam was all around my new bed.

'Can you see it?' I whispered across the enchanted room to my sister.

'Yes,' came her answer, so faint that I knew she was hiding, as I was, under the bed-clothes.

We seemed to share for hours that trance, unable to stir or shriek for help. Gradually, overcome by exhaustion, we disappeared at last from ourselves. After that first night we never saw the flood-gleam again.

Years later, that excitation of the optic nerve became a constant delight whenever I climbed the mountains in the west of Ireland and saw below me rivers and the lakes that no man has made. At night when I closed my eyes, I saw a continual succession of lakes and rivers gleaming beneath shadowy mountain ranges. I was much pleased, as water is a symbol of vision. The Gaelic poets were accustomed to think out their poems beside stream or loch though they perfected the assonantal patterns of them lying on their beds in the dark.

The next day and for many days after that eventful night at Roundwood, there was much for us to explore. Behind Vartry Lodge was a small ravine, topped on the opposite side by a wood which we could not reach. Along the path on our side, however, there were safe spots down which we could scramble to watch the cascades of the rivulet or fish in the pools for sticklebacks. Brushing the hedge beside the narrow path, we came to the gate of the fruit garden which was full of gooseberry bushes, red and black currant, most of them much higher than our mouths. The path led down to the other end of the filter beds and every day we visited the forge there and helped to blow the bellows. Once the blacksmith, with a few quick strokes, made metal walking-sticks for us, complete with crooks, but our delight in them cooled almost as quickly as the metal itself for they were heavy and unyielding. Outside the forge was a huge bank of sand and we watched the men shovelling, the horses drawing the full trucks along the narrow rails to the filter beds.

Among those children left so much to themselves, the moral problem which had disturbed me so much as Valleymount appeared, although mischief itself remained. Mr. Farrell was a low-sized bearded man, powerful and quick-tempered, with a remarkable gift for appearing suddenly out of nowhere. We must have been a constant annoyance to him for he often charged after us in fury especially when we were trespassing in the meadow below the lawn. I was both surprised and pleased by the entire lack of parental reverence which his youngsters had for him in secret. They used a special warning cry whenever they spied him making towards us.

'B.O.P.'

Ostensibly the initials were those of the *Boys' Own Paper*, but in reality they stood for Bloody Old Peter for that was the Christian name of Mr. Farrell. So, as I dashed to safety with May, Jack, Nan and their cousins, I repeated joyfully under my breath those words in full: Bloody Old Peter, Bloody Old Peter.

Even religion seemed to be less rigid in the east of County Wicklow. On our first Sunday, we all walked the mile-and-a-half along the road near the shore of the reservoir to the village of Roundwood. We arrived some minutes late at the chapel and the congregation was standing up for the first Gospel. We stole quietly up the stairs to the gallery. Scarcely had we sat down after the Gospel when the rickety back bench collapsed with an appalling crash. We all slipped away to find other places. Shamefaced, I groped down the few steps to the front of the gallery and found myself beside a tall curly-headed civil engineer whom I had met in Dublin. He was a practical joker and I was always much afraid of his extraordinary humour. But this time he glared at me ferociously as if I had been responsible for what had happened and I was so agitated that I knocked over a large prayer book on the ledge. It fell upon the people below with a noise which might have been a faint delayed echo of the preceding crash. Although we were kneeling again, waiting with bowed heads for the solemn moment of the Elevation, I realized, to my surprise, that the young man's shoulders were shaking not with holy rage but with suppressed mirth.

It was during one of our occasional visits to Roundwood village that I met for the first time a real artist. My own daubs in water-colour faded instantly when I saw him painting on canvas with thick brushes and oils. To make all more wonderful, he had only one hand. The other was wooden and hidden in a tan glove, but somehow he contrived to keep the palette on his forearm. Later he became a well-known painter and did a remarkable portrait of James Joyce's father, a perfect representation of one of our best-known national types, the Drunkard. I met him for the last time in this life on a summer's evening in Dublin at the corner of Earl Street soon after he had returned from a long holiday in Spain. He changed a great deal and his expression was furtive. Glancing around guardedly, he lowered his voice.

'If you hear anyone saying I had anything to do with women, don't believe them.'

He repeated this two or three times and then left me. I felt that he, too, was one more victim of our strange European teaching. Soon afterwards, he emigrated to the United States, where he died under tragic circumstances.

I cannot remember my discovery of the spring or when my secret visits to it became a daily habit. Somehow or other I succeeded always in slipping from the house before breakfast without being missed either by my sisters or the other youngsters. It was perhaps the delicious sensation of that pure cold water on a small empty stomach which began it all. Nevertheless, the fact that I did not tell anyone seems to suggest an obscure imaginative impulse which I did not understand. So, when it was Mass time in the city far away, I glided by the laurels near the gate and went down the path under the embankment, past the fir trees and the spot where the wild bees' nest had been found. Just where the plantation stopped there was a turning on the left, almost hidden by grass under a bluff. Ivy grew down the rock and on the top was a jumble of furze and shrubs. Steps had been cut out of the granite and on the side of the rock was an iron hand-rail. I hurried down but had to be careful for water dripped from the fissures above and oozed across the steps. The path turned abruptly and around the corner was a grotto, hartstongue and other little ferns around it, spring water trickling from a pipe into a rock basin. Superstitiously, I cupped the water in my hands, closing my eyes against the morning dazzle or blinking them sleepily as I watched the far-off woods and mountains in the south-east. Sometimes, when there was mist, the watery light seemed to be coming from a hidden cloud-spring of its own. That little rite which I had discovered for myself and performed exactly every morning gave me a new joy. Nevertheless I forgot all about it until long after when we were struggling one day in class with a poem of Horace, groping through difficulties of grammar packed within every eighth of an inch. Suddenly the words *Fons Bandusiae* shone from the page and I was back once more at that lonely spring, my hands cupped.

However, I was not entirely absorbed in such mysteries for at least on one occasion I behaved disgracefully towards one of the little girls and, so to speak, dirtied her bib. A relative of the Farrells had come to stay at Vartry Lodge with several of her children. One morning, when we were all playing around the doorstep of the kitchen, some dispute started. I had just been sent to a fine Jesuit College and even in first grammar must have acquired some of the snobbery of the place. Turning to the little girl with whom I was quarrelling, I silenced her with a terrible remark.

'Well, at any rate, I don't go to a common National School like you do!'

Some hours later, when I had forgotten all about that tiff, I was confronted by an angry parent. Mrs. Kelly was a small delicate woman with many children, and a few years later, she went into a rapid decline. Pale with fury, that day, she told me what she thought of me, using an extraordinary amount of words as if I were a grown-up. When she had done, she never spoke to me or looked in my direction again during the entire holiday.

Often, in a band, arming ourselves with sticks, we hunted in the woods along the shores of the reservoir with a collie and two spaniels. The excitement of this chase caught us all. Shouts, yelps, furious barks always gave sufficient warning to the rabbits which we startled through the bracken.

One episode comes back to me clearly because of my scruples, for it reminded me of those dire minutes in Meath, when a small boy and I had harried the swine. News came that one of the filter beds was to be cleaned and we were provided with baskets immediately after breakfast, having complete leave to wet ourselves as much as we liked although I did not know this until afterwards. Stalwartly, we boys hoisted our calico breeches, while May, Nan, Elizabeth and the other girls kirtled their skirts and pulled up their drawers as far as they could. We scrambled into the ebbing water, feeling soft sand sinking under our toes. Here and there we dashed in pursuit of the trout, floundering in the shallows, unable to escape from us. We splashed forward, driving them before us and scooping them up between the truck rails. Not being a country child, I felt that our sport was rather unfair. I had a moment of remorse when I grabbed at a great pounder for, as I hugged the slippery creature against me, I almost fancied that one of the metal sea horses on the piers of the gate was alive and struggling from my grasp.

Every evening, we trooped along the gravel, past the french windows, the flower beds and the pear-tree espalier along the wall. The Eyres were not in residence and so we could play on both the lawns. I was the ring-leader for the sixpence I had given my sister Eileen some years before proved inexhaustible and we enacted the fairy tales she had told me as we went down Capel Street past the sweet-shops. This was indeed my second childhood for we acted Snow White, the Babes in the Wood and other such tales. The plantation at the end of the lower lawn was mysterious as we rustled through last year's leaves or crept along the deep mould. As I had company, it was exciting to venture through the darkness as a robber or wicked uncle and then dash out as myself into the twilight once more.

When we came home from the country, I tried to continue those twilight games, but the concrete of the backyard and the few alders in the garden lacked the obscurity of those woods through which we had rustled and there were no lawn slopes down which we could precipitate ourselves. By chance, however, I acquired some austere tales which could be enacted without elaborate set. We were never taken to see our poor relations who lived in Francis Street, but sometimes my cousin Paddy Myler came to our house on an errand. I was fascinated by the old Norman name, Myler, and even then felt its strangeness. I envied Paddy, who could play in the lanes and alleys of the Liberties. Once he brought me a couple of books for the Bairns, with their terra-cotta covers much begrimed. One of them was about the fire-myths of the Maori; the other had tales of ancient Greece. The events were puzzling but one of the Greek legends became a favourite of mine, no doubt because it dealt with the element of water. So I played it frequently with the children who lived next door. The window-sill of the little room behind our scullery was not too high: the chosen one could leap from it through clouds as the winged horse, whose name was too difficult for us to pronounce. The horse galloped around until he was captured and ridden pick-a-back, while in a wild chorus we whirled around with the fuzees which we had bought in Mrs. Carroll's toyshop near Capel Street. The green and Bengal red flares waved through the darkness and then came the supreme moment! Pegasus stamped the ground and from its hard concrete a fountain leaped up, so clear, so dazzling that it might have been one of the hydrants bursting in the street outside. The illuminated matches burnt out and the fountain disappeared in the darkness.

We never went to Roundwood again and years passed before we spent another holiday in the country. Once a year, however, there was a school picnic for the best boys to the Dargle, the Glen of the Downs or some other place in County Wicklow. Often, as I fell asleep, I wantoned in thoughts of those deep shady woods and streams, longing for the day, once a year, when I would see them again. By comparison, the fields of Cabra, on our side of the city, seemed ordinary. Nevertheless I enjoyed those sunny days in summer when I ran with butterfly-net up and down the hillocks near the Water Tank at Liffey Junction. Without any twinge of conscience, I asphyxiated the unfortunate specimens I had caught in a special glass jar full of camphor, and added them, pin by pin, to my collection.

Once as I was chasing a white butterfly, I ran down into a deep hollow after it. A man was standing there in the shadows, squat and with a brown bushy beard. Silently he beckoned me but, as I came towards him, I glanced down and was chilled by instant fear. Then I fled up the slope.

'I've seen the devil,' I exclaimed to my sisters.

They laughed at my nonsense and I was shrewd enough to say no more. A moment later I was happily chasing another little cabbager over our downs, quite forgetful of that sudden meeting with the Evil One. Nature, it seems, can protect us from what is beyond our full comprehension when we are very young. Nevertheless, after that glimpse of future terror, I always avoided those hollows of Cabra.

I can still remember the dreary discomforts of the return journey. The Cabra Road was long and straight so that, as we trailed home wearily, we could see, a mile away, the first terraces of houses. The footpath and the hedgerows which hid the cabbage fields were always thick with dust, but it was pleasant to rest at times in the convenient alcoves made by the patient courting couples who came there in the twilight. The lanes around Cabra were leafy but they were spoiled for me by a plant with a greyish blossom which always made me shiver for it was called Dead Man's Hand. Even the hawthorn blossom which looked so pretty was dangerous and protected from our grasp by more than thorns. In the country the may is known as the fairy tree, but in our city lore its spell was more fearsome for a single branch of it would bring consumption into the home. That dread disease was rarely mentioned directly but we knew only too well all about it. Down Mountjoy Street, beyond the Black Church, opposite the last Victorian residences, was a terrace of small red-brick houses. In one of these, poor Mrs. Brennan had died from tuberculosis at an early age, leaving her husband, an elderly retired policeman, with a large family. One by one, the children went into a rapid decline and followed their mother into the next world.

Eight

I

A FAMILY which has been living in a city for several generations suffers from one disadvantage: there are usually no country relatives to whom the children can be sent for a holiday in summer. However, we had relatives in Liverpool and so I was packed off with one or other of my sisters year after year to England. The journey itself seemed to prove that we must suffer in this world for our few joys. It was exciting to hurry up the gangway, explore the steerage deck, see the capstan, the big ventilators, the anchor chains; but pleasure quickly disappeared as the mail-boat steamed out to the Irish Sea. The waves were always choppy, the air on deck became colder, the gusts boisterous. Soon my sister and I were staggering to the scuppers, leaning over the rail as the ship dipped and rose. At last we had to crawl down below though we knew that we would become worse there. The steerage was grim for the iron sides of the hull were bare and the benches were painted a sickly yellow; the pans into which the unfortunate travellers vomited were of the same appropriate colour. The joints of the gigantic pipes above us were covered with what seemed dirty bandages and the effect suggested a crazy hospital. We lay on a bench or sat groaning while the pans slid as the vessel rocked, and mothers clutched their bawling babies. When the first fit was over, I spent the rest of the time in an agony of dry retching.

Nevertheless, all our misery vanished as soon as the throbbing of the engines changed. We hurried up the gangway into the fresh air and felt that dream-like sensation of the *Cambria* or the *Hibernia* gliding into the harbour at Holyhead. We passed the black-and-green promontories of Anglesey; being near, they looked harsh and cold, unlike the gentle hazing of Howth and the faraway Wicklow Hills which we had left behind. But that early experience, though it left me with a dislike for sea-travel, strengthened my stomach and when it was larger I was master of it. Only too well did I get to know that crossing of the Irish Sea. Usually I travelled by night and, in the steerage, watched our people emigrating or coming back to see their relatives. Most of them were from remote glens and backward places, shabby and rough, subdued or numbed by the strangeness of their surroundings. Their ill-fitting clothes, their little brown-paper parcels and cheap battered cases stirred vague feelings in my mind. Despite myself, I shrank from their uncouthness and felt ashamed of them, yet raged at the historic circumstances which forced them into exile at a time when our new Free State had been established. The wild drinking of fellows who had never learned to hold their liquor like their betters filled me with pity, though I knew that in less than an hour most of them would be reeling and spewing all over the place. Here, indeed, was the floating ark of my kindred.

Whenever I could afford it, I paid an extra seven-and-sixpence, and a slender rope divided me from all that wretchedness of the past and the near future. Those few shillings changed all and as I made my way to the saloon I glanced enviously at the comfortable private cabins. In the saloon all was seemly even when the sea was rough: comfortable basket chairs, small tables, softly shaded lights, obsequious Welsh stewards. Passengers were dressed in their best clothes, the last of the Anglo-Irish still talked loudly and in the corners, priests, on their way to the Continent for a holiday, were reading their breviary or sipping large whiskies. Symbolized by that ship's rope was the separation between the well-to-do and the poor which has been increasing every year in our small republic.

In those far-off days of childhood, I must have spent most of my time at the railway carriage window looking at the Welsh glens and seaside resorts as we sped by, but I can remember only the clattering of the train past suburban stations as we approached the terminus. Our cousins met us at Lime Street Station and in a few moments we saw the long Art Gallery with its rows of steps and the wide square which always seemed to me askew. The Liverpool trams were a dingy maroon in colour, and they had narrow hard seats like those in the steerage of the mail-boat. So in secret I felt very proud of our own cream-and-blue trams and the new ones had cushioned seats even on the top deck. Soon we were rattling and heaving along in one of those despicable English trains through crowded thoroughfares, past the shops, until all got drabber, dustier, and I knew we were coming towards Easby Road, near which Aunt Maria and Uncle Jim lived.

Uncle Jim was an Englishman and a cooper by trade. He had worked for some years in Dublin at Guinness's Brewery and married my mother's eldest sister. Therefore the Aynscoughs were not emigrants and I never met any other Irish people whenever we stayed with them. Liverpool was a city to which thousands of Irish men and women came after the Great Famine and there was also a later migration. The monster meetings held by Daniel O'Connell in the days of Catholic Emancipation were followed by those of Father Matthew, the Apostle of Temperance. Statues have been raised to the memory of this young zealous reformer, whose impassioned oratory moved multitudes and even the stern British Government gave him a pension of £300 a year. But the emotion aroused by his evangelical campaign throughout Ireland did not last and most of those who took the pledge in a moment of mass hysteria soon broke it again. The sudden cessation of drinking was disastrous to the owners of small public houses, for the banks quickly foreclosed. In a year, more than twenty thousand, cast out of employment, had gone to Liverpool and the north of England. The drink and the miserable merriment were back again and as the prosperity of the middle classes increased, examples soon showed that temptation is no foe to faith and celibacy. At Locke's Distillery in the Midlands, it is said that there is a huge Victorian ledger known as the Priests' Book, a register of our betters, who were devoted to Protestant Pot Still.

We never thought of Aunt Maria's three sons and married daughter as being even partly Irish. They had small brown eyes, while ours were large and blue; the boys, indeed, had such sallow skin and black hair that they almost looked like foreigners to us. Moreover they spoke with an English twang and, as we liked our own flat Dublin accent, we thought their speech horrid and derided it when we came home.

Aunt Maria had a little shop at the corner of one of those innumerable side streets through which I wandered freely and got to know so well. There were delightful surprises in her shop and in the others throughout that neighbourhood: bottles, for instance, of sarsaparilla, mysterious in name, yet disappointing because the beverage itself had a slightly medicinal flavour; cream soda, despite its plain name, as delicious as the lemon plait which we used to buy in the village shops in County Wicklow. That sweet was always stale and, therefore, soft – soft as the new fizz.

Every morning, along those side streets, all exactly similar, with their rows of small working-class houses, an astonishing sight was to be seen. Housewives on their knees seemed to be salaaming like frenzied Orientals. They were all busily scrubbing their doorsteps which were of red sandstone and worn down in the middle. Every morning I hurried out to watch the rite and I must have tripped past hundreds of backsides. Those steps shone in their perfection even on dark days, and it was, perhaps, some desire to lessen the grim dirt and squalor which caused all that house-to-house rivalry. Was it, too, some instinctive reverence, in a region of coal and steel, which accounted for the gleaming kitchen ranges in all the houses we visited? They might have been as sacred as the ancient cooking altars at the Temple of Jerusalem and probably were much cleaner since they were closed. Those housewives must have spent much time blackleading, brushing, polishing, saving pence from the weekly wage to acquire the steel pokers, shovels, tongs and fire-dogs. The kitchen range in my aunt's house was always radiant and there were two fire-stools of ornamental steel at each side of it. My mother had been so delighted by these that she sent for one and it shone as brightly in our own home as it would have in Liverpool.

Beyond those drab streets were wonderful regions which I saw at week-ends when Jim and my other cousins were back from work. Sometimes we travelled in the overhead railway for miles along the docks watching the cargo vessels and the ocean ships with their white decks, red, black or green funnels. Once we walked beside a dry dock, gazing up at the largest liner in the world at that time – I think it was the *Baltic*. The great pride of Liverpool, however, must have been the tunnel under the Mersey and I was constantly aware of this triumph of man though, for some reason, I never saw it. Always in our conversation we came back to that mysterious tunnel and whenever I crossed the Mersey in one of the paddle steamers I thought of it below us. We crossed to Birkenhead, to Wallasey and other places with strange names but they were disappointing when we got there. New Brighton, however, was different for it was a holiday resort and whenever we came down to the landing stage which rose and fell with the Mersey tide, I could see far away the metal tower. At New Brighton I had two unforgettable experiences in five minutes: lasting disillusion followed by momentary terror. Outside an Amusement Park I saw on a brightly coloured poster a picture of a giant octopus and paid my penny to see this monster with its writhing tentacles. I passed a canvas screen and found myself alone in a small space of trampled grass. There was a barrel full of water and I peered into it, but all that I could see was something at the bottom that looked like a piece of pickled cork. Being too young to understand the advertising world, I felt that I had been the victim of a mean deception, so when I came out I pretended that I had got my pennysworth. But I was determined to compensate myself and, a couple of minutes later, when we came to the Tower building, I stepped for the first time in my life into a lift. To my complete astonishment, I found myself alone with three Red Indians. One upward glance at those huge immobile figures with long black hair, head feathers, knife in belt, hurled instantly through my mind all the stories I had read about Buffalo Bill, arrow-stricken wagons, shrieking captives. At any moment I felt that the Indians might be tempted to revert to their primitive habits and scalp me. Then the lift stopped and I left those noble creatures, doomed to live by making a show of themselves.

On a fine Sunday, we went to Southport but that trip, so full of little pleasures, ended in the horror which is always near in childhood. Cousin Jim had borrowed bicycles for Eileen and me. We must have lingered among the amusements beneath the Great Wheel and beside the artificial sea-lake, for it was lighting up time as we came towards Liverpool again although that summer evening was still clear. Suddenly a policeman stepped forward in the middle of the road and held up his hand. Eileen swerved very cleverly under his arm and escaped but we were not so quick. To my astonishment, Jim gave a name and address which I had never heard of but the policeman was suspicious and took us to the station near by. Jim winked at me as we were brought in and this gave me courage for I knew that I must not betray him. We were led into separate rooms for questioning and I realized for the first time that I was in an enemy country. Often in County Dublin, when I was cycling with my father, I had seen the R.I.C. carrying carbines and the iron shutters of the barrack windows with slits from which, if necessary, they could shoot down their fellow-countrymen. The awful might of the British Empire, the regiments of Redcoats marching through the streets of our capital – all filled my mind with an historic terror. Two policemen were questioning me. I shook my head, pretending that I had forgotten my cousin's address and, to make matters worse, I could not even remember the false name which he had given. Although I tried to keep back the tears, I would have broken down very soon under that dreadful ordeal, but the door opened suddenly and Jim was brought in.

'It's orl roight, you cawn tell 'em.'

He had quickly realized my plight and come to rescue me. Eileen was waiting anxiously for us at a safe distance and, as we cycled along, I asked Jim why he had told the police that his family had been living at the supposed address for only six months. He explained that a new address would not appear in the directory until the next year.

II

It must have been on another visit to Liverpool that I saw a play for the first time because my eldest sister was with me then. It was so frightening an experience that I have never forgotten it. Often in the evening Jim took us out but, as I was always asking questions, both tired very soon of my company. On one occasion they stole quietly from the house without telling me. Having quickly discovered they were gone, I was determined not to be left behind. Smiling at my own cleverness, I raced down several side streets and, with a triumphant whoop, confronted them in Easby Road. They looked quite crestfallen but good-natured Jim quickly solved the problem for he gave me a shilling and so got rid of me for the evening. My cleverness was only too well punished. Somehow or other I found myself in the gallery of a theatre: I have forgotten the name of the melodrama which I saw although the beginning of the second act is still vivid to me. The scene was a dimly lit drawing-room with a conservatory at the back. A woman came in and suddenly was as stricken with horror as I was, for, in a green ray, she saw, in the conservatory, the ghost of a murdered man, seated there in evening dress. I was used to sheeted spooks in the stories which I had heard or read but that lonely figure so rigid in the appalling green ray made me cold with terror. For years afterwards, I woke up from dire dreams staring at that Liverpool ghost in evening dress.

The young have their own sense of humour and sometimes the well-meaning practical jokes of elders can have unexpected consequences. Life has only a limited number of pleasures and Cousin Jim, yielding to a momentary impulse, deprived me for ever of one of them. On a Sunday evening we had gone to visit his married sister, Winnie, and high tea was served with some style in the small parlour. On the table was a red glass jug which appeared to be full of sugar stick. The white-and-pink gleaming through the glass was very attractive and I longed to have some. Jim pushed the jug towards me in his affable way.

'Evsam Broighton Rok!'

I seized a sugar stick but the moment my teeth met on it there was a rending sound and a sour taste filled my mouth. So, whenever my friends are eating celery, dipping the stalks lightly into salt, savouring, crunching them noisily – since this is permitted by good manners – I experience again to the full that early shock.

Although celery had been snatched from me, I gained in Liverpool another pleasure which has lasted. Old Mrs. Annesley far away in Dublin in her fairy-tale house beyond the flower beds would not have approved of the circumstances. On a chilly evening in that dingy Liverpool purlieu, I was sitting close to the kitchen range and much too near my Uncle Jim. Every Saturday night he was in an amiable mood after a few beers for Aunt Maria, who was very fat and easy-going, accepted the English way of life and took him as he was. On Sunday morning he was once more a model British husband, cooking expertly the roast beef, the cabbage, baking the potatoes, and, what was to us a novelty, the batter of the Yorkshire pudding. On that Saturday night, however, he was worse than usual and almost incoherent. Proud of his strength, he was telling me of some prodigious feat of his as a swimmer and, through the confused maudlin ramble of words, came a continual refrain, which shaped itself at last in my own Dublin speech.

'I've swum the Liverpool Docks.'

Good-humouredly, my aunt, who was serving in the shop, came in a few times and tried to rescue me for it was long after my bed time. But Uncle Jim kept firm hold of me and continually repeated those remarkable words as if I did not believe him.

'I've swum the Liverpool Docks!'

I had never heard the past participle 'swum', and thought it was ungrammatical, but the pleasure which Uncle Jim took in the sentence made me aware, vaguely, of its sound and rhythm. Sleepily, that night I must have felt for the first time the power of onomatopoeia, for that long-lost sentence came back to me suddenly when I read Dame Edith Sitwell's minute, almost mystical analysis of the sound patterns of poems. Had she been with me that night, I am sure that she would have delighted in the texture of the oft-repeated sentence: the long *i* of *I've* and the smooth v suggests a perfect dive without splash, and the phrase itself is actually a thought-rhyme, with *dive.* The *sw* and *m* of *swum* suggest the movements of the swimmer, while the narrow *u* makes us aware of the depth of the dock into which he dived. In *Liverpool,* the liquid *l's* and *r* suggest the gliding movement, while the *ive* is a half-echo of *I've,* and the *oo,* preceded by a mild explosive consonant, suggests both forward movement and floating. Finally *dock,* with its short *o* gives us the feeling again of depth and the initial dental and closing glottal consonant suggest the walls of the dock. They bring us, too, a sense of finality, the abrupt grasp at the granite edge as the swimmer emerges safely, while in the final *s,* with its effective sibilance, we hear the water dripping from the naked flanks of my Uncle Jim.

Nine

I

IT is likely that my early acquaintance with an industrial port was premature for, in coming years, I remembered, with vague uneasiness, those Liverpool by-streets through which I had wandered so often on my own. In my twenties, when I was travelling in a train at nightfall towards Manchester to stay for a few days with an Irish poet, D. L. Kelleher, who was a journalist there, I hesitated to glance from the carriage window. When I did so, I was immediately surprised by the dire vegetation of that terrible plain. As we passed factories surrounded by slagheaps, dumps, debris of inextricable scrappings, I found myself watching for the stunted bushes, the oily gleam of stagnant pools and half-dead streams. Along the distant, darkening horizon was the glare of blast furnaces; pitchy smoke was rising from tall rows of stacks; soon, despite myself, I felt the infernal grandeur of all that ugliness.

The next day I was still aware all the time of that nocturnal fire and dirt for the heavy cornices and ornamental sculpture of the banks and great commercial buildings in Manchester were black with soot. I hid for a couple of days in the Art Gallery with its great collection of pre-Raphaelite paintings. On Sunday, however, while my friend was at Mass, I ventured into a large public park. The trees were bare, dank, for it was late autumn, and the sky was smoke-grey. I walked despondently in that solitude staring around at the scant muddied grass, thinking that most of it must have been kicked away by footballers. Suddenly there was a ray of sunlight and, in the distance, just over an incline, I saw the top of a triumphal arch. It must have been quite new for it seemed to be of pure Carrara marble. Overjoyed by the unexpected beauty of all its whiteness not yet defiled by soot, I hurried towards it. As I came near, mists hid the sun and the illusion was gone: I was staring up at a granite entablature thick with the excrement of seagulls.

On the following afternoon, I set out on my journey southwards and, despite my ardent belief in Irish republicanism, was determined to enjoy my holiday in London. The November sunshine came brightly through the carriage window. In a few hours I would see London again for the first time since I had passed through it as a lad of seventeen, and in my pocket were letters of introduction to Alice Meynell, G. K. Chesterton, Clement Shorter and other writers. It was some years after the first great war, and the younger English poets were astir with hope and excitement. They were turning, like the realistic novelists, to the new pleasures of fact. They wrote of stock-yards, muddy football fields, drab parks in drab suburbs. I was sorry that I could not watch from the train window the cinder wastes and factories which had inspired Wilfrid Gibson, the poet of the Black Country.

But it was difficult to muse in that railway carriage, for the Englishmen around me were beaming with friendliness. All that I had heard about this taciturn, phlegmatic race was evidently untrue. These men were strangers to one another; yet after a few tentative remarks about the weather they were soon talking together with surprising gusto. The small, dapper man who sat opposite me might have been a Dickensian character despite his appearance – he talked with such volubility and gaiety. Suddenly he leaned over and placed something in my hands. To my astonishment, it was a pack of cards.

'Would you mind shuffling these, sir?' He spoke as if he were asking a tremendous favour.

Puzzled and yet flattered by this extraordinary request, I made some awkward passes with the cards and handed them back to him. He seemed completely satisfied and thanked me deeply. He proposed a game of cards, and the other men joined in the game. He asked me casually to take a hand, but I declined, being ashamed to admit that I did not know how to play. However, the game proved to be simple: guessing one of three cards known as the Lady.

Francis Thompson, in one of his essays, has warned writers not to live their poetry. I forgot this literary advice when a shy young man sitting beside me took part in the romantic game of Spotting the Lady. Why should I not take part also in this masculine sport, seeing that I had only recently written a devil-may-care lyric about a famous Irish gambler?

Had I the diamonds in plenty, I would stake
My pocket on kings that walked out with Queen Maeve
Or wager the acre that no man digs in Connaught,
And after the drinking, I would cross my soul, there,
At the bare stations of the Red Lake.

I would risk a handful of silver with these foreigners! My recklessness was justified, for I doubled my stakes, trebled them, quadrupled them. The young man was as lucky, and notes were pressed into our hands with extraordinary rapidity. I knew for the first time the excitement of gambling. In the sunlight and tobacco smoke that hidden lady was appearing and reappearing. She was a benefactress of letters, she was bountiful as Mairead an Einigh, surpassing the Lords of Ely. But suddenly all that wealth vanished again. I was drawing on my own holiday money. Suspicions were stirring dimly in my mind, and they were echoed by the young man, for he whispered to me:

'They're card-sharpers, but we'll get back our money. I'll mark the card.'

Slyly he eared the queen during some shuffling. Conscience-stricken, I hesitated, but the thought of beating these card-sharpers at their own game was irresistible. We spotted the marked card, but it proved to be spades. As we gambled desperately the lady seemed to have dozens of disguises, and every ear was thumb-nailed. For the first time I noticed the man in the corner seat opposite me was not playing. He was signalling to me with his eyes, but I was too confused to read the message. The lady was gone. There was nothing but the huge pocket, into which my holiday was disappearing.

They gave me hearts as my share of the dealing.
But the head that I love is not red and it is not black,
And I thought of the three that went over the water
And the earth they had when they brought Deirdre back.

The train stood at a station. The men hurried out of the carriage. The young man turned to me in great distress.

'I've got to get out here. I'm going to a new job, and I haven't even my bus fare.'

I had two half-crowns left. I gave him one, and we shook hands in our mutual unhappiness. The silent man was still in the corner seat.

'I tried to warn you,' he said. 'But I could not say anything, there were too many of them. One of them slipped this to me as he was going out. It's yours. You may need it.'

He handed me a ten-shilling note.

'But the young man?' I was trying to palliate my own foolishness.

'He was the decoy.'

Staid, taciturn travellers crowded into the carriage. But I avoided the man in the corner. Might he not be another decoy? And might the plot not deepen?

The friends with whom I was to stay in London met me on the platform. I assured them that I had a most pleasant journey. But my literary visits in London meant long journeys on foot, and so I never met Alice Meynell, G. K. Chesterton and others. However, I discovered one satiric pleasure for myself. If I sat long enough on a free seat in any London park a highly emotional Englishman was sure to step from the sunlight and confide his troubles to me. He was always the son of a baronet. There was a legacy coming to him through difficulties from Canada, hints of jewels and diamonds. I listened agreeably to the traditional story, knowing that I was completely protected by my empty pockets.

II

James Joyce is no longer regarded as a spiritual enemy of his own country. So great is his fame that his books can be bought openly in Dublin although those of the majority of Irish writers, including three of my own, are banned. In the Summer School held annually at University College, Dublin, lecturers expound his work to foreign students and, among local Joyce experts who write about him, is an eminent Jesuit. It is even said that the record of Molly Bloom's once notorious monologue, spoken by an actress with an attractive Galway brogue, has been found useful in the confession classes in several ecclesiastical colleges. When the great Belvederean shook the dust of Dublin streets from his canvas shoes and went into voluntary exile, he took with him a young Galway woman but, in his revolt, refused to regularize the union.

There is, however, in Ireland an offence which is regarded with even greater horror than adultery. Modestly and without quite realizing the consequences, I committed this offence against my country and soon found myself unwillingly on the other side of the Irish Sea. At the time of the said offence, I was English assistant at University College, Dublin, and I had been appointed after some hesitation for the authorities there were rightly suspicious of young poets. The post had previously been held by a poet who was executed by the British as one of the leaders of the Easter Week Rising. The college authorities at that time were firm supporters of the Irish Parliamentary Party and were opposed to the Sinn Fein movement. They felt, therefore, that the National University, which had always been known for its cap-in-hand loyalty, was disgraced. I was determined to behave myself. Certainly the savour of the pottage was good and I sniffed in it those spices which had come from afar. I knew that I was on trial and so I was not surprised when, after my first year of lecturing, the Professor of English Language and Philology invited me for a private little talk to Leeson Street. As we sat in the gloomy parlour, I glanced at the gloomier oil-paintings of the saints of the Counter-Reformation. This Jesuit father was an elderly little man with a rosy, yet withered face, a fine musician, with a sensitive appreciation of poetry, but frustrated, for he had little knowledge of Anglo-Saxon. After some desultory conversation, he came at last to the point with that slyness which is caused by years of total obedience to others. He suggested that, instead of writing about pagan Ireland, I should attempt a religious theme. It so happened that I had been reading *The Death of Adam*, a spacious poem, by Laurence Binyon, and it occurred to me that the lonely death of Moses on Mount Nebo after his vision of the Promised Land would make a complementary theme. Unfortunately my imagination was stirred by the various pleasures of polygamy which had been permitted by God to the patriarchs under the Old Law: and, to make matters worse, I was tempted, like the Israelites themselves, by the variety of polytheism and so displayed an undue interest in Baal, Ashtaroth, Dagon and other idolatrous figures. The experience was worth while for I had learned that it is very difficult to sell the sub-conscious self. Moreover, the poem seemed a parable of our own lean centuries. In the first lines appeared that symbol of my childhood, the papal grapes, disguising itself so cunningly, that I did not discover the nexus until I woke up suddenly from a dream last night.

Soon afterwards I became infatuated with a young woman writer who had come back from the Continent at the outbreak of the war. Despite some rivals, I was soon a constant visitor at her flat. She was older than I and secretly I was tantalized by her past for, in one of her poems, she hinted that an Austrian officer had committed suicide because of her. The implication of cruelty made me uneasy at times but, when she lit two candles and let down her hair, I could not resist the pale gleaming of her face. She had ignored the new fashion and her black tresses reached almost to her knees: hidden poetically in their shadow I was well-nigh lost. Margaret had advanced opinions and, having some small private means, was independent and could express them freely. She was a fervent admirer of James Joyce and was writing a novel, which was to be entitled *Portrait of the Artist as a Young Woman.* In it she described her own early religious experiences and they were like my own for she, too, had hated the insidious questioning in the confessional. I liked in particular the episode of her first disillusion as a sensitive child. She was so awed by the quiet voices of the Dominican sisters and their graceful white robes that they almost seemed heavenly spirits to her. Then one day she tip-toed into a forbidden part of the convent, little knowing how she would be punished both for her disobedience and her curiosity. She looked down from a window into a cobbled courtyard, saw on a clothes-line a hideous row of bloomers and burst into tears because of their enormity.

Eventually we decided to marry secretly in a registry office and tell no one about it for some time. But the simple guile of amorous couples had been long since anticipated both by the Catholic and Protestant bishops of Ireland during the reign of Queen Victoria, and we had completely overlooked the question of banns. The Dublin Registry Office in a side street near the Quays was drear and forbidding. The floor of the lobby was bare and we sat waiting on a wooden bench, realizing at last why the Registrar was known in popular parlance as 'The Beggars' Buckler'. In a few minutes we were informed that we must state the church which we had attended for one month before the date of our intended union or cause to be published in a local newspaper the name of the house or houses at which we had knelt in private worship. We chose the first alternative, which seemed to us quite safe, but in a few days anxious clergymen were hurrying to the flat in which Margaret was living. We persisted, nevertheless, in our design and, at the end of nine months, my University appointment, which was a yearly one, was not renewed. I realized that the authorities were embarrassed for it was only after two months of waiting that I learned indirectly that I was no longer on the staff. I could not blame them for I had committed too grave an offence and the penalty, in effect, was banishment.

Unfortunately my marriage proved a failure for it was only a marriage in name and lasted less than a fortnight. So I left Ireland to seek work as a book reviewer in London. In the horrible gloom and fogginess of those first weeks there, as I wandered through the crowds, I saw all distortedly as if I were a French or Belgian writer of the 'Nineties. I murmured to myself the lines of that poem which Verhaeren had written in London, lines which were strangely prophetic, for he met his death at a railway station.

Gares de suie et de fumée, où du gaz pleure
Ses spleens d'argent lointain vers des chemins d'éclair,
Où des bêtes d'ennui bâillent à l'heure
Dolente immensément, qui tinte à Westminster.

On Saturday evenings I passed by the crowded public-houses in the poorer districts, repeating to myself, in a mood of self-pity, his sonorous exclamations.

Et ces châles et ces gestes de femmes soûles,
Et ces alcools de lettres d'or jusques aux toits,
Et tout à coup la mort, parmi ces foules;
O mon âme du soir, ce Londres noir qui traîne en toi!

I had found lodgings in a grimy street off the King's Road in Chelsea. It was difficult to write in that small back room, for the large front room on the same landing was occupied by an Australian, who had fought in the war, his wife and a baby that was always crying. They kept the door open, perhaps to let the smell of cooking escape. As the ex-soldier never went out, I found it difficult to get to my room for he was always on the watch. He was a tall discontented young man and he always depressed me for he talked continually of a coming war, so greatly did he miss the excitement, the danger, the bloody excitement and the cheering crowds at the railway stations. The other lodgers were decent tradesmen but I met them only at our Sunday dinner in the kitchen for, when I came down to breakfast, they had long since gone out to work. Their only grumble was that someone in the neighbourhood kept cockerels and I dared not confess that, when I was awakened by the crowing at dawn, I was delighted and pretended to myself that I was far away in the Irish countryside. Our landlady was a fat, kindly widow but I had to face the same problem every morning. She took an amazing delight in the latest murders which she had read about in the Sunday papers and discussed their gruesome details with me. As I had great difficulty following her quick Cockney speech and knew nothing about those stranglings and choppings, I had to nod gravely or utter an occasional exclamation of dread. Once, when I had succeeded in changing the conversation for a few minutes, I discovered that she had spent all her life in the same neighbourhood and had never even crossed the nearest bridge over the Thames. Her secret dream was to cross that bridge some time and visit Battersea Park, which she could have reached in a quarter of an hour. I promised to go there and tell her about its wonders. I had been affected by her dream and, when I got to the Park, saw the wintering trees, the bare ugly stretches and railings, glanced at the nearby electric works and slum streets, I hurried away. The next morning, drawing on my early memories of the Phoenix Park, I made my landlady happy for I knew that she would never cross that bridge.

The fare in my lodgings was rough and ready but generous in quantity. Unfortunately my stomach, which was used to pure Irish food, shrank from the shop eggs, the coarse bacon, the margarine and, on Sunday, the chilled beef and the frozen mutton. After some weeks, I decided to find lodgings elsewhere and set out for Victoria. Pimlico attracted me for its name had been given to a poor district of small houses in Dublin which was slowly decaying under the walls of the mighty brewery there. Hurrying down a side street, I saw a card in a window. A neatly dressed woman in her thirties opened the door and, as she smiled pleasantly, I had a glimpse of the clean oilcloth on the staircase and the polished brass rods. I knew instantly that I was in luck and I was not disappointed. The back room on the first landing cost only ten shillings a week. There was a gay counterpane on the bed, a table with a cloth of the same colour at the window, where I could work, and a gas fire. It would be pleasant to hurry out for breakfast to one of the small cafés or eating houses which I had noticed on the Vauxhall Bridge Road.

On the Saturday evening, I came back eagerly to my room about eight o'clock to write my first review, for I had been given a few books to do by Robert Lynd, who was Literary Editor of the *Daily News.* When I had switched on the electric light, I decided not to pull down the blind for, beyond the backyards and the rooftops, I could see a wide reach of sky. I had been writing for some time when I noticed that the window opposite mine was lit up. I took no notice but after about ten minutes I happened to glance towards it again. I might have been in an obscure quarter of Montmartre for, on what seemed to be an illuminated screen, I saw the silhouette of a young woman making lascivious gestures. As I watched that shadowgraph, I thought of Baudelaire, but this black nude was not African, for her figure was slim and graceful. At times she moved slightly and the silhouette became blurred, then, in a moment or two all was clearly defined again. At first I was puzzled until I realized that the large window was either of muffed glass or had been covered with a paper transparency and, looking closely, I could see that the performer was at that moment drying the small of her back. Being young, I had no wish to be a voyeur and I quickly pulled down the blind.

As chance would have it, I returned on the next evening to my room at about the same time. I had scarcely opened the door and was still fumbling for the switch when I noticed that the bathroom window opposite was lit up again, but this time I had come in the middle of the performance and was much surprised. The shadowed one was bending down and at the same time balancing herself on her left leg while her right knee was raised. It took me half a minute to realize that she had her foot on the bath-stool. I was indignant at her stupidity in making a show of herself and wondered whether a shadow could be indicted but, having yielded to the temptation, I waited until she had given a last pat to her hairpins and the light went out. Then I decided to go for a brisk walk.

As it was a Sunday evening, that ill-lit street in Pimlico was deserted and the curtains of all the houses were drawn. At a short distance in front of me, I saw a mongrel ambling along by himself and could not help noticing that he passed the lamp-posts without stopping. Despite his dejected appearance, it was obvious that he had some purpose in his little mind. So, in order to distract my own, I decided to follow him. Soon we came to a crossing with several corner shops closely shuttered. He hurried over the road towards one of the shops and I could see him on his hind legs licking at something in the shadowy doorway. He remained there for a minute or so, then, much refreshed, turned and padded back again down the street. I crossed the road and found that the shop was a dairy. There was a brass tap in the door and a slot for pennies a few feet from the ground, no doubt so that small children might be able to reach it when they were sent out after closing hours by their mothers for an extra half pint of milk. The device was ingenious but the washer must have become defective for, when I stooped to investigate the tap, I found that a minute drop kept forming on it.

Later that night, as I lay drowsily in bed, I thought less harshly of the careless young woman who lived in the next street. I fancied that I was walking along the pavement and saw her coming out of the house. She was fair-haired, dressed in a close-fitting tailor-made costume and I knew her at once by her figure. Somehow we almost collided and, as I turned to apologize and was raising my hat, she smiled so pleasantly that we both began to talk at the same time. At this point the second page of my novelette blurred and I was fast asleep. I woke up some time later from a happy confused dream: I remembered seeing from a hotel bathroom window the damp foliage of the woods at Avoca and kissing my wife on the bare shoulder. I sat up in the darkness for I could detect distinctly the fragrance of lavender. For a moment I was puzzled and then I remembered some more of my dream – it was the fragrance of bath salts. As I dozed again, I became aware that someone was in the bed beside me and I felt on my left arm the gentle touch of a finger-tip. I lay there, scarcely breathing, and then I groped cautiously and found I was mistaken. Next moment I was wide awake but I could still feel that gentle touch. When I moved my arm it was still there and gradually the horror of what was happening reached my mind.

As I rolled from the bed and stumbled through the darkness to the switch, I seemed to be a child again in Liverpool. I remembered how my father at the quayside had jocularly warned Doto and me to beware of the bugs there for we had often heard of them and they had become a minor myth to us. Our sub-conscious fear of them, sea-sickness, a strange room, must have made us both uneasy for we woke up that first night in a simultaneous nightmare. I saw my sister's face pale in the moonlight, her dark, lovely eyes flashing with terror. We set up such an Irish shrieking that my poor aunt and uncle rushed into the rooms in almost as great a fright.

When I switched on the light in Pimlico I saw a bug on my forearm.

The next morning, after many restless hours of broken sleep, I explained to my landlady that I had been recalled unexpectedly to Ireland. That evening I was at Euston with a single ticket in my pocket, waiting on the No. 13 platform, which all our exiles have known so well.

Ten

I

ALTHOUGH my grandfather had not been very practical, my mother seems to have inherited her business sense from the Browne family. She invested the money which she had saved patiently for many years in a little house property. After the death of my father, by careful buying and selling, she achieved a small income. I doubt whether a single line of my verse ever meant anything to her but I was equally incapable of following her complicated mental calculations or explanations of mysterious clauses in old leases. Soon after I had come back from London, she suggested in her distant manner that I could devote myself entirely to my writing if I wished to do so. It was a tempting offer and there was always the paradoxical example of Bernard Shaw. Had I been content to wait for the uncertain moments of inspiration, warm in my pockets a few shillings every week, and remain a celibate like so many young Irishmen, the experiment might have succeeded. But despite reconciliation with my mother I could not live too near her will and wanted to be independent again. So, being restless and still disturbed by the failure of my secular marriage, I decided to go back to London. I did so with regret for, despite the emotional havoc of the Civil War and its immediate miseries, the Irish Free State was just beginning and hopes for a small independent literature with its own standards of criticism were astir. W. B. Yeats was living in Merrion Square; A.E. was editing his new liberal weekly, the *Irish Statesman*, and encouraging the younger generation of poets.

Back in London, I was climbing office stairs again with little results, and then, one Tuesday afternoon, in a mood of recklessness, I entered the large building of an important Sunday newspaper, and pressed the lift button. I stepped out at the first floor, gave my name at the counter and, in a moment or two, without the slightest hesitation, I was shown in to the Literary Editor.

'Make yourself more comfortable,' said Mr. Godwin, and he chuckled as I stammered shyly and sank back into the huge armchair which he had pushed towards me. The next moment he was moving past the review books on his magnificent desk with a rapidity that astonished me, for he was almost rotund.

'And now what can I do for you?' He swung round with the same rapidity on his revolving chair and waved a thick, dimpled hand. The gesture seemed to imply that anything I wished for in his spacious office, with its mahogany bookcases, ample carpet and filing cabinets, might be mine for the asking. He looked more like a businessman than the literary editor of a London newspaper; for he had a large flaming cheek, and tiny brown eyes that watched me sharply. But he smiled benevolently and scarcely waited for my hesitant words, so eager was he to anticipate all my wants.

So I wished to review books for his paper? He would be only too pleased to help me, but there were certain difficulties in the way. Many distinguished writers contributed to the columns which he edited, and his reviewing list was full. He looked grave, and in instant depression I heard the grim sound of traffic in the street below. But Mr. Godwin was smiling once more and rubbing his hands as he gazed at me with affectionate concern. He was deeply interested in poetry and I must tell him all about my work – indeed, he was always anxious to help young poets. He mused, as I spoke; at times smiling to himself, at times nodding sympathetically. He would give the matter due consideration, and meanwhile, I must not be downcast. He stopped in the middle of a cheerful sentence and looked up reproachfully. His secretary had come very quietly into the room, and was waiting anxiously to speak to him. Mr. Godwin jumped up in great distress from his revolving chair. He was so sorry . . . an urgent appointment . . . he had almost forgotten it. I had already reached for my hat, recognizing the polite makebelief which means that all is over.

But I had wronged Mr. Godwin, for he came to the door with me and put his arm round my shoulder.

'Drop in again next Tuesday, same time, and we'll have another chat.'

Punctually on the next Tuesday I was shown into the office, and Mr. Godwin met me at the door with a second mighty handshake. On his desk I saw with great joy several neat piles of new books in gay and serious wrappers. They were within arm's length of me, but, as Mr. Godwin's geniality increased, they shone as remotely as the hopes of heaven. As he leaned back, chuckling over an anecdote which he had just told me, I pointed with quiet desperation to a book on top of one of the smaller piles and said that I would like to review it. He glanced towards it and replied with some severity: 'That is going to Mr. X.' He mentioned the name of a well-known critic. His quick answer had made me suspicious, and, with the sudden cunning of despair, I indicated another book, choosing one at random in the middle of the largest pile. I was certain that Mr. Godwin did not know which book I wanted, but he immediately mentioned the name of another celebrated reviewer to whom it had been promised.

'Send me a postcard with the names of some books you would like to review.

I clutched my hat and rose sadly from the huge armchair. But once more I had wronged Mr. Godwin in my thoughts, for he patted my arm at the door and chuckled knowingly.

'Next Tuesday, same time. Don't forget.'

That day week the clerk at the counter informed me that the Literary Editor was very busy but would see me for a moment. Mr. Godwin was walking up and down in the office dictating a letter to his secretary and I was alarmed by his gloom. He drew me aside and muttered: 'I got your postcard, but I'm afraid we can't review those books. Their publishers don't advertise with us.' His tone seemed ominous and I stammered as when we met for the first time. In my foolish ignorance, I had touched the hidden chill of English commerce, and I heard the clatter of lift-gates. But Mr. Godwin had dismissed his gloom for the moment and, with gigantic good nature, accompanied me to the lobby.

'I'll look up some books for you myself.' His paternal hand was already on the frieze of my overcoat. 'Next Tuesday . . .'

'Same time?'

He nodded and smiled me away

Almost two months had passed and still the generosity of Mr. Godwin remained celestial. In the darkness of my future it was a busy ball of fire, and late into the night, as I sat in my drab bedroom, I tried to discover the meaning of its mysterious combustion.

One Tuesday I had to wait some time in the office, for he had been delayed at lunch with a successful novelist. His face was glowing as if he had left the grill room in a great hurry. Indeed, it positively glittered as he chuckled and laughed so that I suspected that he was intoxicated. But that was the only occasion on which he kept me waiting. How, indeed, could I explain his eagerness to see me so regularly when he always sent me away empty-handed? On wet evenings as I trudged through the dirty streets beyond Chelsea to my lodgings, I hated his cheerfulness and brooded morbidly over it. I knew that he did not read books, and that his sight had never been dimmed by them. Yet, despite myself, I felt that there was something of genius in his exuberance, so fully had he escaped from the taciturn silence and frigidity of his fellow-countrymen into the talkativeness of the past. But strange suspicions shook me, for I knew that my own frustrated expectations held me in his power. In that minute experience – was I enduring one of the millions of merry pinches in which a conquering race indulges? I remembered my childhood years, when my elders were tormented by political hope and despair. How often had not Home Rule been held before their minds, and then snatched back again at the last moment! Patriotically I stayed away for two weeks, but yielded once more to curiosity and hope.

Mr. Godwin reproached me for my absence, and then pointed to the increasing piles of Christmas books on his desk with an encouraging chuckle.

'I want you to do an article for me next week, so be sure to come again on Tuesday, same time.'

When I reached the great newspaper building on the next Tueday I noticed vaguely that the outer office was crowded. But I walked briskly and determinedly to the counter.

'I'm afraid you'll have to wait, sir, all these gentlemen are before you,' said the clerk, with a nervous gesture.

I turned and saw a number of young men waiting patiently in a long queue. There must have been at least twenty-five of them, and in my agitation it seemed to me that their faces were pale and strained with anxiety and wonder. I glanced at that row of young reviewers as if I were seeing in a number of hateful mirrors the multiplied reflection of my own features. Then I fled from the newspaper office into the busy street.

Some weeks after Christmas I learned the truth. Late that

afternoon the unfortunate Mr. Godwin was removed to a lunatic asylum.

II

'You must go and see Shaw,' exclaimed one of my friends enthusiastically in his broad Scottish accent. 'Yes,' urged the other, 'he is sure to give you better advice than we can.'

I was touched by the solicitude of these two middle-aged men for I knew that they themselves were powerless to help a young author who had just arrived in London. Both of them wrote verse but they had never had the slightest success, for one was still an ill-paid assistant in a large drapery store and the other was a minor clerk in a suburban post office. When I was seventeen and had just matriculated, I met them by chance at Chilbolton, a little village among the Hampshire downs where my sisters and I were spending a holiday with family friends. Herbert Grant and George Stevens were both Socialists and I was surprised by their kindness and unselfishness, for at school we had been often told that Socialism was wicked. I went for walks with them, past fields of sanfoin, which I saw for the first time, and out along the ancient Roman Road, bordered with meadowsweet, and they talked most of the time about poetry. Grant had known William Morris, and told me about those crowded gatherings, where all were equal, at the poet's home in Hammersmith every Saturday evening. In a fortnight they had to return to counter and desk, but they left with me Swinburne's long poem *Tristram of Lyonesse* and the early romances of William Morris. Lying at the edge of a cornfield in the August sunshine, I read on and on, comprehending little, but dazed and delighted by the movement and music of the words. It is probable that today the young experience the same mysterious pleasure from the harsh obscure poetry of our time with its disassociated images.

When I met Herbert Grant again in London, I saw regretfully that he had shaved off the grey beard which gave him so distinguished an appearance. Poor man, he feared that he would be dismissed if his employers noticed that he was growing old. Both of my friends regarded Shaw with veneration as one of the leaders of the Socialist movement. I had read his plays with considerable nervousness, being alarmed by his wit and analytic power. But it was in vain that I mentioned to these humble admirers my suspicion that he had little sympathy with poetry. Anxious not to betray my country by word or gesture, I did not tell them of my instinctive feeling that our famous Irish exiles had always been concerned with their own advancement.

So, on a wintry afternoon, having yielded to the importunities of these unknown poets, I stole past the *Nation* office on the first floor of the Adelphi Building, in which Bernard Shaw had his town flat. A cold light shone down from a high narrow window as I went up the stairs and the ornamental railing was chill when I stopped for a moment and put my hand on it. My courage was disappearing and I hoped that the great man was not at home or would be too busy to see me. But if he were there and willing to see me, what could I say to him? Would he dismiss me in half a minute with a smile and a witty remark that would leave my ears tingling? I was about to retreat when I remembered how disappointed my two friends would be. I hurried up the stairs with renewed determination but, when I had almost reached the last landing, I stopped completely astonished by what I saw. The landing was guarded by a stout wooden gate with a formidable row of iron spikes. On the gate itself was a notice board with a forbidding word painted on it in large letters: PRIVATE. As I stood staring at this unexpected obstacle, a thought struggled dimly to reach my consciousness. It came at last. I was back in my childhood looking at an illustration in an old copy of the *Pilgrim's Progress*, which had often held me in fascinated terror. It was a picture of an ogre's den and I could see once more the lamentable human bones strewn on the ground. Although I feared the searching mind of Shaw, I knew the allegorical implications were absurd for was it not notorious that he was a vegetarian? But in that gloomy light, I felt very small and was filled with foreboding. I felt that a Socialist who could avail himself so thoroughly of the rights of private property would not welcome an intruder. Glancing once more at those spikes, I stole down to the street

Later, I saw Bernard Shaw for the first time at a debate in the Kingsway Hall and it could be described as a memorable occasion, for G. K. Chesterton, Hilaire Belloc and Lady Rhondda were also on the platform. Never had I suspected that an English audience could show such enthusiasm and respect for the craft of letters and, as I watched the eager faces all around me and heard the expectant murmurs that spread through the hall, I felt glad that I, too, was a writer. Hilaire Belloc was in the chair – and it was obvious that he had lunched well for his face was flushed and, when he rose to introduce the speakers, he grasped the edge of the table so firmly that I seemed almost to feel the immense effort of his will. G. K. Chesterton opened the debate and the young Church of England clergyman on my left was so excited that he almost jumped up from his seat every time that he applauded. Indeed I was certain that in a few months he would become a convert to Catholicism. Suddenly, to the surprise of that large audience, Hilaire Belloc rose abruptly from the chair as if he had been insulted, left the platform and marched grimly down the central passage. Chesterton continued to speak, but his words had become meaningless. Two thousand ears were listening to the violent swish of the swing doors, the clatter of the historian's feet on the tiled floor outside and the distant banging of two more doors. Chesterton continued to speak but all were listening to the silence beyond. Then once more, to our relief, we heard the banging of those distant doors, the clatter of the French military boots, the violent swish of the swing doors. The poet-historian marched up the central passage and took the Chair again.

When Lady Rhondda rose to speak, she had to wait until the audience finished clapping; then, leaning forward, Shaw exclaimed in a loud genial tone: 'Lady Rhondda, go in and win!' The use of that familiar war-time expression so delighted the audience that they clapped again for almost half a minute as if to show their appreciation of Irish wit. Truth to tell, I had begun to realize that the enthusiasm of the audience was indiscriminate. None of the speakers at that meeting said anything of importance and I have forgotten the very subject of debate. Even Shaw was content to accept the general homage without making any effort to earn it with some brilliant remarks. Nevertheless, it was pleasant to hear his cultured Dublin accent unspoiled by a single London inflection and watch him so much at ease as he spoke to us from that platform. Quite unexpectedly, in the middle of a trivial sentence, he said something which sent a thrill through me, something which I have never forgotten. In his colloquial way he was using the trite expression Tom, Dick and Harry, but he varied it, and what he said, in passing, was Tom, Dick and Sally Noggin. Had it occurred to him as he was speaking that the proverbial saying belonged to the past ages of masculine aggression and did he feel, as author of *The Intelligent Woman's Guide to Socialism*, that the phrase should be amended? Was that tiny deviation due to a chance recollection of his early days at Dalkey, which is only a few miles away from the village of Sallynoggin, now a suburb of Greater Dublin? Or was he remembering a local expression of the time? I cannot tell but I felt that I was perhaps the only one in that audience who had noticed the reference and for a moment I seemed to share in secret a little joke with him.

Years later I was to see Bernard Shaw for the second and last time. I happened to be travelling from Oxford on a Sunday afternoon in summer and there seemed to be very few people on the train. When the train reached Paddington, I glanced from the window and saw the sunlight shining through the glass of the arched roof on an empty platform. There was not even a porter in sight. Although I did not delay, I was not the first off the train. A few yards in front of me was Shaw walking briskly despite his age. I was puzzled for a few moments and then I remembered that the Malvern Festival had just ended. The railway carriages from his train must have been attached to ours at Oxford or some other junction. A taxi quickly drew up to the station kerb but, instead of getting into it, Shaw stood waiting for somebody. Long since, I had learned to appreciate his plays and had tried to adapt some of his technique in writing verse-drama. I had even come to the conclusion that his guess at the meaning of existence was better than some other guesses which I knew only too well. I was seized by a powerful urge to go up and speak to him and it seemed to me as if the very Life Force were trying to make me do so. But I had outlived the impudence of youth and I felt that the strict conventions had their own place in the striving universe. I hurried past but when I had gone a little way, I could not resist glancing back. Shaw was still standing there but he had drawn himself to his full height as if he were posing before an invisible camera: tall, lithe, with noble features and handsome grey beard, he was an extraordinarily impressive figure. The unworthy thought crossed my mind that he was expecting press reporters to arrive. I glided behind a pillar and waited to see what would happen. The Malvern passengers were getting out of the carriages at the end of the train. As if by one accord, they drew themselves up in a line against the carriages, suitcases in their hands, gazing reverently at that magnificent figure in the distance. Then, as if all were accomplished, the playwright got into the taxi and it drove away. Through the narrow window at the back I could see his lengthy nape growing smaller and smaller until at last it disappeared in the distance. I lingered on the platform after the passengers had gone but I was still staring, in a disturbing vision, at all that mighty neck.

III

Book reviewing as a profession seems to be disappearing and I was fortunate, therefore, in catching the last of its great Fleet Street tradition and in knowing and learning its teamwork from such literary editors as Bruce Richmond, Robert Lynd, H. M. Tomlinson, Desmond MacCarthy, Leonard Woolf, R. Ellis Roberts, R. Scott-James and others. In particular I owed much to Sir Bruce Richmond, who corrected my early efforts and often rearranged my sentences for me. He was a man of high principle and had a very difficult task as Editor of the *Times Literary Supplement*, for all the reviewing was anonymous. On one occasion, he had published a long article by that fine poet Lascelles Abercrombie about another poet, and he told me of his horror when he discovered later that both were not only close friends, but shared the same lodgings. It was an intellectual exercise to learn to write in different styles: to be dignified in Printing House Square, precise and somewhat Anglican in Covent Garden, sceptical and outspoken in Great Queen Street, familiar in a popular way both at Ludgate Circus and in the Strand.

I lodged for some time in Bloomsbury and contributed reviews to the same periodicals as the brilliant experimentalists there. I never met any of them, and suspect that the popular legend about their exclusiveness had some truth in it; but I cannot prove this, for I was scarcely aware of their existence. I was absent-minded in those years, because my thoughts were always hurrying back by themselves to Ireland. In consequence I knew nothing of the latest ideas, which were causing such a stir all around me. Nevertheless, in some dim way, I must have realized that I was breathing in a very rarefied atmosphere, for a few months ago, I came upon some old reviews of novels which I had contributed at that time to the *Nation*, and found, to my astonishment, that I could scarcely recognize them as mine. Each of them began with a brief disquisition on the aims of the contemporary novel and they were so compressed, subtle and elliptic in their metaphysical notions and abstractions that I could not grasp their meaning – if they ever had any.

Alarmed and surprised by the increasing emigration of our people to the Welfare State, our bishops warn us against the dangers of 'pagan' England. Having already yielded to the Celtic paganism of our literary revival, I found that my mental temptation was of a different kind and whenever I passed the Protestant bookshops around St. Paul's, I quickened my steps. On a quiet Sunday evening, I found myself drawn there almost against my will and, venturing round a corner, I saw the Dean of St. Paul's hurrying across the pavement to a pillar box. At that time, Dean Inge was writing a weekly article in an evening newspaper and, as he had a large foolscap envelope in his hand, I wondered if it were another of his theological attacks on the older Christian establishment. Shortly afterwards I was to learn from an odd experience the danger of private judgment.

IV

In the corner of the eye there is a tiny trickster that is older than ourselves. As I wandered through many purlieus of London, this mischief-maker enjoyed himself as hugely as a foreign body of minute dimensions under the lash. His mirth increased whenever I passed a drab church or dissenting chapel in a side street. For always I averted my glance from the religious placard behind the railings. But irregular bits of Biblical quotation jigsawed before my conscious sight and I hurried along the pavement as if invisible proselytizers were trying to touch me on the shoulder. In the dim days of infancy we are taught only too well the differences between creeds, but in the years of discretion we can change historic hatreds into a passing shudder or thrill of holy horror. One day I resolved to confound the nuisance in the corner of my eye, and I hurried resolutely to The World's End.

The strange name of that cheerful and dirty place beyond Chelsea had attracted me for many months. There, inside and outside blackened shops with their dusty signs, second-hand furniture was piled; peering through a sooty shop window, I could see chumps for sale; in the next shop window eels from the Shannon were steaming. In an eating-house which I frequented, there was always, for a few pence, a prompt portion of pease pudding, and I knew fairly well the pawn-shop round the corner, quiet as a confessional with small wooden partitions of coarse yellow varnish.

At The World's End there was a church which had a peculiar gloom of its own, for it never knew the sunlight. But it had a large placard with a boldly printed text which I had avoided for some time. I stopped before the placard and stared impudently at the text. The words proclaimed that a righteous nation shall spread and possess power in this world. Despite myself, I was possessed by what seemed spiritual joy and my mind filled with a new knowledge. I had been brought up in the belief that all mortal activity was vain, and that nothing mattered but the pursuit of eternal pleasure. Now all was changed. I saw as in a vision a cheerful, unequal, workaday world; shops crammed with the good things of earth, great scaffoldings, ships a-building, turbines revolving – a busy nation, ruling far lands and seas, and populating the next world with brisk and efficient citizens. The spiritual exaltation lasted only a few moments, for I realized that I had been tricked into full concupiscence of sight by the curious little devil in the corner of the eye.

But one sunny afternoon in July, as I sauntered towards South Kensington along a quiet respectable street, a voice rang out through the air in terrible protest against that cheerful religion of the workaday world. 'Behold the Lord will come with fire, and with His chariots like a whirlwind, to render His anger with fury, and His rebuke with flames of fire.' Alarmed by those ancient words, I glanced along the rooftops, but could not discover the hidden proselytizer, although his voice had become more menacing: 'For by fire and by His sword will the Lord plead with all flesh: and the slain of the Lord shall be many.' At that moment I noticed that a stout middle-aged woman had stopped at the corner of the street and was looking up towards the sky. Then she turned hastily and came back down the street with an expression of virtuous indignation on her face. Immediately after that, a young woman reached the corner, and looked up in the same way. She hesitated, wavering on her high heels, and then fled past me in distress. Astonished by the remarkable conduct of the two women, I hastened to the corner.

At some little distance in the next street there was a large mansion of flats, and on the top balcony I saw a white figure gleaming in the sunlight and gesticulating towards the sky. As I came nearer I saw that the figure was a tall elderly man with silver hair, and, moved by the impassioned sincerity of his voice, I scarcely realized for a few seconds that he was completely naked. Remembering the tormented torso of martyr and saint, there seemed no incongruity in that pure state of Nature. Certainly, a visitor from abroad, ignorant of those words of doom, might suppose that this was just another eccentric Englishman who had discovered in his bath the forgotten tenets of the Adamitic heresy. The commissionaire of the mansion flats, who was standing in the roadway, seemed to think so, for he was calling to the tenant above in tones of shocked respectability and his arms were raised in prayerful entreaty.

'Oh, Mr. Sotheby, do go in. Please, please, Mr. Sotheby, do go in.'

I tried to attract the attention of the commissionaire, but in vain, for, despite his heroic inch of war decorations, he had begun to hop from one leg to the other like a victim of St. Vitus' dance. I ran up the steps to give the alarm, and a determined young man suddenly appeared from nowhere and joined me. We dashed past the lift and up the stone staircase, past the mezzanine, past the second floor until we came to a small dark corridor.

A merry outburst of dance music met us, and the small corridor was filled with elderly ladies and gentlemen. They looked dazed as if they had been awakened from a gentle afternoon nap or interrupted in their quiet reading of detective fiction. They were all speaking in hushed, scandalized voices, and I fancied that I caught their murmurs.

'Oh, poor Mr. Sotheby! What can have happened to him? It's dreadful! Is somebody ringing up? Mr. Sotheby . . . Poor Mr. Sotheby!'

Muffled by the locked door of the flat came the voice of Mr. Sotheby, and joyfully, triumphantly rising above it, the sound of a band playing an old-fashioned waltz. As the young man rushed at the door, a policeman came running up the stairs. The lock yielded, and in a moment we half tumbled into a pleasant room filled with sunlight. Music blared at top pitch from a wireless cabinet, and I felt that we were struggling through a gigantic waltz to that open balcony window.

Mr. Sotheby was about to hurl himself from the low balustrade, but we caught and dragged him back. As the poor creature struggled against so many hands, the great religious poetry of remote centuries shrieked from his lips like horrible profanity, and that crazy waltz, lightening its way from Bournemouth, danced in every corner of the sunny room.

V

Some years before the last great war, my second wife and I had taken a couple of rooms for the sake of cheapness in a drear side street near the Seven Sisters Road. I found it difficult, however, to work when our baby had to be in the same room or the next, so we decided to look for a place in the country, where I could work undisturbed and our one-year-old could have plenty of fresh air. Every writer dreams at some time or another of living quietly in the country, of straying along field-paths and listening to the birds in the copses. Edmund Blunden, Walter de La Mare, W. H. Davies and other poets sang the praises of their countryside through every season. So I looked forward to the pleasures of an English shire.

We had been lucky in finding an old house hidden among trees in Hertfordshire. It was owned by an eccentric couple, but we had two storeys all to ourselves. Every evening, long after sunset an ugly red glow appeared in the south-east beyond the oaks and hornbeams. It was the glow of peace-time London, more than twenty-five miles away, and even when I turned my back on it and watched the moonlit meadows, I knew that I had not entirely escaped from the great capital.

At morning all was different. Daffodils lingered in the long grass outside our windows. The hedges were wild and the house and outhouses were dilapidated. It was pleasant, however, to come back from the spick and span highways, the neatly trimmed hedges and faultless fencing. Even the little wandering lane leading to the gate of the old house was a disgrace. It lost itself in a wilderness of thorn and scrub-oak, and there was a great patch of thistles which grew to a prodigious height as the summer increased. When I touched those thistles, in passing, they swarmed like the tenements of ancient Rome. Innumerable flies darted from every storey with angry buzzing noises as if I had disturbed Beelzebub, master of all insects.

Katherine Tynan had advised me to write always in a summer-house if I wished to live long. I remembered her advice the moment I saw the small summer-house between the last trees and the meadow's edge. Every morning, as I hurried across to the summer-house, there was some new surprise. Grebe darted through the grass to the pond under the willows. Young partridges, who had escaped from one of the neighbouring estates, scurried away with a great flurry of wings. Sometimes a pheasant ran, nodding, into a hedge. Under the eaves of the summer-house were mud-daubed rounds, and I studied with interest the tiny kraal of the swallows. It was pleasant to pause at the end of a scribbled line and hear the rustling of wings as the parent birds came and went. But in a few weeks the summer-house was filled with a minute pandemonium. All day, as I struggled to write nature poems, the fledglings screeched. When their parents arrived and clawed at the eaves, there was a terrific outburst of hoarse twittering. When their parents left again, the din was even worse.

One sunny morning there was a new and unexpected menace to my peace of mind. 'Cuckoo,' shouted somebody in a loud, derisive tone just outside the summer-house. I dashed out, angrily, believing that some small boys were playing a trick on me. But hedge and meadow were empty. I had understood from several celebrated poems that the cuckoo always keeps at a distance. But this cuckoo seemed to delight in shouting just beyond the door-step and sill. I could never see him, but I felt as if somebody had hidden in the grass an alarm clock which was liable to go off at any moment. Finally I fled back to the house with my books and manuscripts. But here, owing to my own folly, I had other callers who were as persistent. Three ducks, to whom I had thrown occasional morsels, were there. They had prodigious memories; for they quacked hopefully most of the day outside my window. Neither bribe nor threat could keep them away.

Waterhens, stoats, newts and nightingales seemed the more

important population of that hidden corner of a shire. Ten square miles of demesnes were hedged and fenced from the common eye. The few residents in the locality went up to the city early in the morning and returned, tired, at twilight. It was significant that the last native and his large family were social pariahs. Only at the door of their tumble-down, fairy-tale cottage could be heard the last burring of an ancient and perishing dialect. This outcast lived mostly by his gun, and he had to be a dead shot, for cartridges were costly. Moreover, every cartridge meant a stew or traditional dish. He fed his family on rabbits, wood-pigeon and pheasant, and he was expert, too, with springs and snares. Dainty and shocking meals were eaten in that cottage, such as lark-pie and blackbird pudding.

At nightfall I longed, as an exile, for the melancholy peace of my own Celtic twilight. The barn-owls glided and glimmered from the tall trees. They were silent killers, but they murdered to music; for nightingales sang in the thickets below. One nightingale clung always to a spray at the edge of the orchard, and sometimes I could see him silhouetted against the moon and watch that small, throbbing throat. But when the nightingales had stopped, from far and near came the discordant chorus of the screech-owls. Long after midnight, when Nora and the baby were fast asleep, I was awakened a few times from fearful dreams by a strange cry that seemed to come from the poplar outside my window.

The hideous cry of that unknown bird of prey lingered in my mind even on sunny mornings in the orchard. As the three ducks wandered through the grass with busy gobbling beaks, I fancied I could hear the thin shriek of young frogs, caught as in some fable of Aesop. But one evening the orchard was suddenly filled with delight again. Under the apple trees there appeared from nowhere a tiny dancing cloud of ghost-moths. Here, at last, was a theme for a nature poem. I followed the flight of the ghost-moths who had escaped so gaily from their leaf tombs. But suddenly hundreds of red-spindled insects darted from the trees and began to massacre the moths. After that, the orchard became for me a place of violence and death.

There was one creature who had escaped all harm. He was so old that he was a legend to the elderly couple who owned the house. This was a rudd who lived by himself in a small deep pool overshadowed by beech and oak. As the heat of the sun increased and the water sank in the pool, I could catch a glimpse at times of that ancient fish moving about in the weeds below. One hot day I came to the pool for shade. But the fierce sun rays had already been there. The water was gone, and on the dried earth the poor rudd lay dead.

Eleven

I

VICTORIAN parents always found some model household in the neighbourhood as an example to their own erring children. In our case it was the Geoghegans, who lived in a three-storey house just round the corner at the top of our street and took in lodgers. We hurried past that house very often on our way to the Basin, which was always a little surprise to us: it was a small square pond with a narrow footpath, high railings, two summer-houses and a lonely swan. Occasionally, however, we were brought to see the model family in order that we might be impressed by all its goodness. Mr. and Mrs. Geoghegan were remarkable for the sweetness of their expression, the gentleness of their voices and their deep piety. They sat opposite each other in their armchairs and smiled so benignly at us that we felt they had been murmuring prayers before we came into the room. Their two daughters and sons were as affectionate, Mary, Rosanna, Alphonsus and Michael. Indeed the entire family was always dearesting and darlinging itself. Mary, Rosanna and Michael waited attentively on their parents, doted on their words, kissed them whenever they were going out somewhere and on their return. All this seemed strange to us for somehow or other we were convinced that only English families were demonstrative in this way. Moreover, despite her admiration for the Geoghegans, our mother was quite different. When we said good night to her at bedtime, she turned a cheek to us and we gave it what is known as a 'nun's kiss'. But the Geoghegans seemed to be entranced by their own tenderness. Rosanna was soon to take the veil and Alphonsus, as we knew, was already destined for the priesthood. Indeed, as extra money was needed for this, Mary, who was a National School teacher, had to give up her own wish to be a nun in order to help in finding the necessary extra money. Moreover, Michael, who was the eldest, was still a clerical student in a Liverpool college. We liked Michael the best of all, perhaps because we only saw him when he came back during the holidays or because he seemed to us more independent in his manner. Years later, indeed, we discovered that the family was not entirely perfect. Michael had been once in disgrace. Several students in their final year in Maynooth had been discovered smoking and, *horribile dictu*, Michael had been among them. As this was strictly against the rules at that time, they were all expelled. Michael was advised by some friends to go to Rome and my mother helped to contribute some of the necessary money, though she could ill afford it. However, all went well and soon Michael was permitted to join the English Mission. Unaware of his temporary fall from grace, we regarded him with some awe for we knew that, when he was ordained, he would take part in the great movement to re-convert the English.

Although we really did not like Alphonsus, we were all enthralled, despite ourselves, by his voice for he was a well-known boy soprano. Every Sunday evening Doto played the piano or accompanied me as I fingered my way through a sonata or a chilly arrangement of an Irish air by Esposito. Kathleen recited 'The Song of the Shirt' or some other favourite recitation, and our family friends applauded. Then my father sang one or two of Moore's Irish Melodies in his sweet tenor voice. His favourite was 'Oft in the Stilly Night' and he sang it so sadly that we almost wept to hear. When he came to the words 'Some banquet hall deserted', his tone was so desolate that he might almost have had some premonition of his last year of illness when, despite his popularity, none came to visit him. On those rare Sundays when Alphonsus visited us, all was transformed. He always brought his music case with him and, while my sister played the accompaniment, his clear treble voice rose unabashed, so pure, so holy, that we seemed to be in church. I envied him his gift for he sang without the slightest difficulty, while I had to make my own notes on the violin, feel for them through minute divisions of every inch, practice every day for hours after I came home from school. Yet Alphonsus had only to open his mouth as wide as he could and the notes soared upward to the chandelier, filling our parlour with astonishing melody. To make matters worse, Alphonsus was petted and flattered wherever he went. He sang at Charity Concerts, on special occasions at convents, and was even invited by numerous friends to spend weekends in the country.

One day, my sister ran in with the fearful news that the heavenly voice was gone. Alphonsus had been singing in a Sodality Choir when, suddenly, it broke. I was well used to the ordinary mishaps of violin-playing: the silk string snapped, the catgut couple became even more stringy and dirty and I knew that they would soon break. Sometimes when I chalked the lower key and did not turn it tightly enough, the copper string would rumble and grumble. The bow scratched, squeaked, if I rosined it too much. But the dropping of that pure treble into the bass clef disturbed and frightened me. It could not be a punishment from heaven for Alphonsus was without blot. He accepted the catastrophe without a murmur. Indeed his social activities increased; he was invited everywhere for all his friends were sorry for him and even when he went to the seminary, he spent most of his holidays on a round of visits.

Our acquaintance with the Geoghegans ended as suddenly as that heavenly voice. My mother, in her forthright way, must have detected in their piety some flaw or excess which displeased her. Our visits ceased and we heard no more at breakfast or supper time about that model family. No doubt Mr. and Mrs. Geoghegan sat in their armchairs, smiling sweetly, kissing and being kissed by their adoring offspring, but we were not there.

Soon afterwards, my mother found, for my especial benefit, a model of virtue, which was to last for many years until its unexpected shattering. The model was Willie Moran, who was completely unaware of my unworthy detestation of him. His sister, who had brought him up from infancy, was one of the apple women at Nelson's Pillar. My mother always dealt with her in order to help the good cause for Willie was to become a priest. In rain and shine, Mary sat all day long among the other stall-holders there, selling her apples, oranges, plums, greengages, bunches of flowers, except when her sister Jane took her place so that she might go home for a meal. She devoted herself to the task of paying for Willie's education at college. Every spare make, wing, tanner, or bob went into a tin box and the savings were slowly changed into silver and sovereigns. At the age of fourteen. Willie went to college at Newbridge and constantly I heard of his progress at his studies. He passed all his examinations, though he was not a brilliant student, and eventually was transferred to a large seminary at Tallaght. Then came the news that Willie was suffering from a slight deafness.

Although many were the prayers that were said in convents, in back rooms in Great Britain Street and in our own home in Mountjoy Street, the ailment got worse and we waited anxiously. Then one day Willie appeared in our house and started to attack the Dominican Order so violently that my mother could not stop him. Still in his black clerical clothes, the angry young man told us what had happened. Because of his increasing deafness, he had been flung back in his early twenties into a world which he had rejected so completely as a schoolboy. He could not become a priest despite his vocation and all the savings of his poor sister had been spent in vain. How could one tell him that he should accept the Will of Heaven, explain to him that great institutions could never have lasted for centuries unless the mere individual counted for little in the general good? In his dire spiritual state, Willie rushed from our house and we never saw him again, but I was too moved by my mother's humiliation to exclaim: 'I told you so!' and I remained silent.

II

Among those about whom I wondered much as a child was Mrs. Carney. Whenever I was brought to her little house at Stonybatter, I rarely saw her copious children for most of them were playing down the street and the two new babies were asleep upstairs. In three successive years, she had had three sets of twins and I could not help being puzzled. Mrs. Carney was our family tailoress and I spent my first few years at college in constant apprehension lest the boys from the high-class suburbs should detect a woman's hand in the cut of my breeches. I envied them the splendid shop-suits which they wore and was surprised at their carelessness for they pulled or dragged each other by the collar or lapel during recreation in the quadrangle as they swooped and swept down in predatory bands. I went with reluctance to Mrs. Carney for those yearly fittings and occasional alterations. Sometimes, when the invisible twins started bawling, Mrs. Carney hurried up the kitchen stairs. These stairs had no rails but were boarded in and somehow their oddness contributed to the mystery beyond them. Although my mother was usually with me, I always felt uneasy, on the defensive, when Mrs. Carney came too near me, for this thin wiry woman breathed in a queer way because of the pins which she held in her mouth during the fitting. I could feel the blunt edge of French chalk as she made rapid strokes in the cloth, patting and holding it across my chest. The edges of buckram rubbed sharply against my neck. Her small brown eyes above the aquiline nose were as bright as the needles she used for racking; the faint odour of onion peel came and went as skinny hands darted up and down me; I never knew where those busy fingers would be from moment to moment.

My dislike of these intimacies was due to something that had happened to me in the backyard next to ours and given me a fear of women. On a holy day of obligation, I had called at the back door and Mrs. Hannigan, tall, red-haired, handsome in a long black dress with sequins on it, came in answer to my rap. She told me that Paddy and the other children were at Mass. I happened to be in my Fauntleroy suit, and suddenly she called me a little dote and as I was turning away, gave me an immodest pinch, which left (I suspect) a lasting mark. Years after, when I was staying in Hampshire, that mark was deepened. My sisters and some others were going for a walk on the downs and I was following them with a comely English girl, who was to be married in ten days time. She was so happy, so cuddlesome, that I was surrounded by her glow. Suddenly she put an arm around my waist, squeezed me so tightly that I could scarcely breathe and then, slipping down her hand behind, gave me the same immodest pinch.

Sometimes, when my mother was still talking with the tailoress, Mr. Carney came home earlier than usual for his tea. A powerful, broad-shouldered man, he spent his days coupling bolts, hammering iron plates. Not long afterwards, his wife discovered from some accidental remark made by a fellow-worker that his wages had been increased for over a year and he had told her nothing about it. He had kept the extra money for his drinking at the week-ends. She had toiled day and night at her Singer sewing machine in order to help to support their large family and she was stricken by the meanness of his betrayal. She turned her back on him in bed and there were no more twins. In vain did the local clergy admonish her, point out that it was her duty to obey her husband, in vain did they warn her that such obstinacy might cause him to commit sin. That little dressmaker refused to heed them, defied the Fathers of the Church as if, in her ignorance, she was aware of the long martyrdom of women throughout the centuries. She served her husband's meals, washed his shirts and gansies, but never spoke to him again. In later years, when her sons and daughters were at work, she prospered and came to live near us in a highly respectable terrace on the south side of Dublin. The couple aged together, but the twins, who had not yet been married, had to be the go-betweens. The unfortunate Mr. Carney paid dearly for that unkind act in the far past and did not even escape the miseries of old age. His wits softened and, impelled perhaps by a remaining dread of Purgatory, he was liable, whenever he could, to hurry out of the house at an early hour in his nightshirt and, much to the embarrassment of the entire neighbourhood, had to be led home again from the Church of the Three Patrons.

III

An only boy, who has three sisters older than him, must be aware of an eager daily life different from his own, near and yet remote as story. I knew, for example, that Kathleen, when she was my age, used to steal pennies at home, hurry to Berkeley Road Chapel with them and light candles at the shrines, so much did she enjoy the glitter and pity the empty spikes on the brass candle frames. So whenever I knelt and said a prayer at the shrine of St. Anne or St. Joseph, I remembered all her little temptations. Often my sisters were busily mending or recovering their satchets with pieces of silk and satin. I hovered nearby, hoping to have a glimpse of the tiny bit of wax in each of them. That wax came from the great Easter Candle in Rome and every bit of it was so holy that the nuns who made the satchets dared not touch it but had to pick it up on the point of a needle. The satchets were worn by girls under their blouses and were known as 'Agnes stays'. The word was puzzling and seemed to me slightly immodest for I did not know at the time that it was the local plural for *agnus dei.* When other girls came to the house, I was excluded from the feminine mysteries as completely as if I were in ancient Rome. Always my sisters hurried upstairs with them to the bathroom to tittivate and do their hair. I could hear them, laughing and gabbling there and often, to my disgust, pulling the chain.

Before I was old enough to go to school, I envied my sisters who set off every morning to Stanhope Street Convent. I heard so much about the nuns there that I knew most of them. The Rev. Mother, Mrs. Gaynor, was very grand and rarely to be seen unlike Mrs. Norris, stout, plain, good-natured. The long delicate fingers of Mrs. Nesbitt indeed were in our parlour for she taught drawing and had given the finishing touches to Doto's pictures. These were crayon copies of the Dying Stag and other Highland scenes of the Victorian era and my mother was very proud of them in their white frames. Mrs. Nesbitt was tall, handsome and, for this reason perhaps, was very severe, despite her artistic inclinations, on the sins of the looking-glass. I wondered frequently why the nuns were called Mrs. although they were not married, but such was the custom at the time among the Sisters of Charity: a tribute to the Penal Days.

Sometimes, on their way home from Stanhope Street, past Blackhall Place and the Bluecoat School, my sisters called with a message to the sweet-shop owned by Ellen Keogh, who was one of our family friends. It was a fearful experience to go there despite the presents of toffee and liquorice stick which Mrs. Keogh gave them, for they had to pass Smiley's laundry, which belonged to a Protestant Society. I had heard so many stories about small children being kidnapped by the proselytisers that I was content to admire safely at home the courage of my sisters who dashed past that place on their way to the sweet-shop.

Later, when Doto, Eileen and Kathleen were sent as boarders to the Presentation Convent at Stradbally in Queen's County, some loneliness must have stirred my mother, so often was I brought out by her on visits to friends, clad in my velvet suit with its cuffs of deep cream Limerick lace, my white socks and patent leather shoes with buckles. During the holidays I heard much about Stradbally, but of the nuns there I can only remember Mother Angela because Kathleen was her favourite. She wanted my sister to give her golden ringlets to Dear God but she remembered my grandfather's teaching when she sat on his knee for she never wanted to become a nun. I was always hearing about the goodness of the Presentation nuns and of the meals which were as wholesome as ours at home. Every morning the boarders had not only porridge but a boiled egg and as much bread and butter as they wanted. In winter they were given cod-liver oil to strengthen their little chests and sulphur in the spring for their spots and pimples. There was a walnut tree by the river which became legendary to me because I had never seen one and the youngsters climbed it in autumn for the nuts. Some of them had even discovered where the gardener hid his key and they used to steal into the orchard past vegetables and fruit trees to the apple loft and help themselves amply. The Presentation nuns seemed to us kinder than those in other orders for there was a jocose saying in our Dublin neighbourhood: 'The Sisters of Mercy have no charity and the Sisters of Charity have no mercy.'

At last came the great day when legend became fact and my father took me down to Stradbally to visit my sisters. Much to my disappointment, I saw neither the walnut tree nor the orchard with its locked gate. Instead I was shown in the grounds a great oak, in which was a battered doll which some pupil had thrown perhaps in spite. I gazed at the wretched thing in confusion for when I was very small I had sat in a small room behind our scullery and solemnly broken a large doll belonging to Kathleen in order to find out how its eyes opened and closed. For years she had mourned that loss and found it hard to forgive me. On the Sunday morning, there was quite a commotion in the small hotel at Stradbally when my father came back from early Mass for my clothes were still in the bedroom but I was missing. There was a search high and low and my father was frantic with anxiety. Eventually I was discovered fast asleep in the depths of the immense feather-bed in which he had left me.

Later on, when two of my sisters went to the Training College at Carysfort near Blackrock, Dublin, my double existence was intensified. Being older, I had become more aware of the rich exotic emotion of our religion. I took a luxurious pleasure in the foreign saint names which nuns assume at their profession, for such seemed to suit their mysterious robes and veils much better than if they had been called Sister Ryan, Sister Murphy, Sister McQuaid. I liked Sister Alphonsus, gentle old Mother Gonzaga, and I simply adored Sister Francis of Assisi, so tall and handsome for, needless to say, Kathleen was her pet. Whenever there was Confirmation at the National School in Carysfort, the community prepared a feast for the visiting bishop and other guests. On such occasions Sister Francis of Assisi would bring my sister cakes and other dainties or even hide her in a pantry with a gorgeous plate of trifle. I liked Sister Chrysostom, also, because she taught Doto music in the advanced class and regarded her as the best pupil. But we all hated Mother Attracta and I need hardly say she was squat, ugly and had a red tit-nose. She was very cruel to the poor little postulant, Sister Francis de Sales, though she was so pretty in her black cap and shoulder cape. Like other novices in their first year, Sister Francis had to perform menial tasks as a discipline in humility. Cross old Sister Attracta followed her about throwing bits of beeswax on the floor so that she had to polish the boards over and over again. Even in the chapel Mother Attracta snatched the flowers which she was arranging in the vases. Sister Francis de Sales was always crying and eventually left Carysfort and went to another convent.

Lay sisters were rarely to be seen for they did not even serve at table and so they still remained to me vague shadowy figures. Lay sisters are mainly brought up in orphanages and so, being without dowries, can never aspire to a higher rank. They are the silent service despite all the clatter of basement kitchens, the scrubbing, moiling, toiling, boiling, frying and baking. In these times of uncertainty and baby-sitting, only the religious domestic service remains satisfactory. Perhaps in the far future a memorial will be raised to the Unknown Lay Sister and a minute given to the centuries of their self-effacement and devotion. No doubt their lot is easier now for most religious institutions have anthracite stoves, electric cleaners, floor polishers, washing machines and other modern improvements.

Best of all I remember the spacious class-room on the first floor of the training college with its windows looking out on the long avenue. The girls clustered at those windows to watch the arrival of the young lay teacher who taught mathematics to them. He was very tall, thin, excessively shy. He had a foreign name like those taken by the nuns in religion. When the girls espied that solitary figure in the distance coming along the avenue, they laughed merrily, waving to him with their handkerchiefs and blowing mischievous kisses. They laughed the more as he came nearer, awkward, blushing, not knowing where to look. Even in class they took advantage of the unfortunate foreigner, who said dis, dat, dose. He stammered and stuttered as they stood up in turn to ask him ridiculous, impossible questions and was helpless when they boldly passed notes from desk to desk. The continual noise and interruptions became so bad that eventually a nun had to remain in the classroom in order to keep discipline. I had so often been amused at hearing of the pranks played on young Professor de Valera that I was very surprised when I heard of him again a week or two before the Easter Week Rising. It may be that such early trials and tribulations helped him later to face sternly the sights of enemy rifles, address huge crowds, find his way through the horrors of political dissension and strife to emerge clearly again before most of our windows as the National Hero.

IV

Dublin parents had much difficulty even during the reign of Edward VIII in concealing from their offspring the weaknesses of an older generation. Of course they could not always resist their own humour and play off their knowledge against our innocence. Everytime I was brought to see 'Auntie' Dowdall, who had a small shop at the corner of Benburb Street, the same little rite was repeated. I was asked what I would like to have and, knowing what was expected of me, I replied, 'I want some of Auntie Dowdall's medsin.'

Everyone laughed, including Auntie herself, as I sipped a spoonful of that warm liquid for I was much too young to know that the cheerful old lady was a brandy addict.

The problem of the venerable Mr. O'Duffy could not he solved, however, with a smile. He had once been a fashionable dentist who had failed despite his remarkable skill and his consulting rooms, when we knew him, were above a chemist shop in Great Britain Street at the shabby end of Rutland Square. He believed in saving teeth and I was taken by my mother to have mine scraped, drilled, filled. Only on one occasion he had to pull out a molar, which could not be saved – and I was given gas. I took seven brave breaths, heard a faint roar and found myself in the room below waiting in dread to be given gas: I woke up in the dentist's chair, mouth full of blood and water, the acher gone. My mother was a firm believer in Mr. O'Duffy's revolutionary methods, listened patiently as he explained time and again the reason why teeth should be saved. When he began to denounce the other dentists of Dublin, my mother grew uneasy for he always concluded by railing against the nuns throughout the length and breadth of Ireland. Vainly she nodded in agreement, tried to placate him and changed a conversation which was unfit for small ears. I did not understand what he was talking about but I was puzzled to see that old white-haired man trembling with rage as if he were palsied. It takes us many years to learn that the passion for justice and the welfare of all, once it has been aroused, is the deepest one in mortal life. Later I discovered that Mr. O'Duffy had a large practice in religious institutions and devoted most of his time to the task of saving the teeth of the children in them. But he lost that practice because it was cheaper and quicker to have teeth extracted and so his life's mission was frustrated.

Half-way down the street in which Auntie Dowdall lived was the mill-store owned by Mrs. Mary Lee, who was a devotee of the whisky bottle. I cannot forget that genial fat widow for she was the innocent cause of spoiling for me one of Shakespeare's lyrics before I learned it in class. I happened to be at a school concert in Terenure Convent and suddenly the children on the stage began to sing: 'Mary Lee, Mary Lee, shall I live now under the blossom that hangs on the bough.' There was a constant joke among our family friends that Mrs. Lee should marry a wealthy widower who was as fat as she was. Everyone laughed, even my mother, whenever this preposterous match was mentioned and I was always shocked for I had arrived at the age of bad thoughts and there seemed to be something indecent in the double-bedding of this enormous widow and widower. Mr. Maloney was also as fond of the bottle but, being a publican, he went only occasionally on the razzle-dazzle. These outbursts did not matter very much to us when we were living in Mountjoy Street, but later, when we were living in St. Alban's Terrace on the highly respectable North Circular Road, his visits became a serious problem. We had prospered; two of my sisters were National School teachers and my mother was dealing in house property. So in emulation of old Mr. Cummings, retired publican and city councillor who lived near the Phoenix Park, we had Axminster carpets in the two drawing-rooms, large china cabinets and gilded mirrors, expensive German piano and other secondhand splendours from the many auctions, at which my mother bid expertly. We had, too, in the semi-basement, a sunny breakfast-room with much silver on the sideboard which my sisters polished every week, and we were all proud of the white wall-paper with its pattern of large red damask roses. Sometimes, however, as we were having our tea downstairs, forgetful of the rattle of the trams, we would hear an unusually brisk clatter of hooves, jingle of harness bells, and then an outside car drew up at the kerb. My mother became anxious and, in instant obedience, my father rushed out to help down the much inebriated Mr. Maloney before the neighbours were aware of his condition. We could not, however, conceal the deplorable spectacle from Miss Rooney, the elderly spinster who lived next door. Small, rosy-cheeked, she never sat near a fire but spent most of her time, winter and summer, at a window, watchful, censorious. It was difficult to persuade the mighty reveller to come quietly and my presence helped to delay my father's efforts for I was sure to be on the spot. God-blessing me, patting me on the head, Mr. Maloney fumbled among the change in his capacious pockets to present me with half-a-crown.

V

At a tender age I was well aware of what has now become a national problem – the danger of bad books. Sometimes there was a remarkable silence in our home and I could almost hear it for it was like the soft sound of dusters. I knew instantly that one or other of my sisters was in disgrace once more; another wicked novel had been found by my mother under bolster, mattress or in chest of drawers. The writers of these books seemed to be foreigners and often I heard the dread names of Ouida and Marie Corelli. I was much puzzled by the name of one of the forbidden works for it was entitled *The Sorrows of Satan.* On such occasions I shared deeply the guilt of my sisters for I remembered my own peeps into the Douay Bible: the strange story of Lot's two daughters, the illustrations which depicted naked men and women.

Little did I know that my own turn was to come in my student years. As a stern defender of the Faith, my mother could detect at a glance all forbidden knowledge. Many an unorthodox book disappeared into the closed range in the kitchen; the damper was drawn out, *The Descent of Man*, Arnold's *Literature and Dogma*, Renan's *Life of Jesus*, and other works set the soot a-smouldering in our flue. Even Francis Newman, the younger brother of Henry, did not escape censure and his drastic examination of Christian

Evidences went up in smoke. Needless to say, I was not present when my mother was engaged in such Catholic action.

Only once have I witnessed, quite by accident, the destruction of a bad book. During a holiday in the north-west, I became acquainted with an elderly distinguished lawyer and his wife. She was younger than he and without children but she was of an affectionate nature for, when she cycled along the little roads of that wild coast, her pet dog sat solemnly in a carrier basket. On a sunny morning at the end of September, I happened to call at the guest-house in which the three were staying. When I came in, the wife was alone in the parlour and for a moment she seemed to me a different person for all her pleasantness was gone. Her face was grim and she was clutching a poker in her hand. Blazing on the turf fire was a new six shilling copy of *Thais* by Anatole France.

Nowadays a column of black smoke rises at times above Leinster House when hundreds of books which have been examined by our Censors are committed to the Government furnace.

Our output of books for spiritual reading is now enormous, but in the early years of this century we had sometimes to depend in our home on works by Protestant writers. I remember in particular several novels about ancient Judea by a Victorian clergyman, one of which was entitled *Prince of the House of David.* In turn, my erring sisters read these out to us, chapter by chapter on winter evenings. In them the coarseness of the Old Testament was avoided and the sentences, though large and long, were seemly. I was vaguely disturbed by the vacillations of Saul and the sinfulness of David but I knew that mankind had fallen and I shared my mother's distress. My mother had a deep sympathy for that small race which had suffered even more persecution than our own and, among her friends, were several old Jewish families. As I listened drowsily to those tales of the Jewish kings and moved in their palaces, I was aware patriotically of our own ancient kings, though all I knew about Brian Boru and Malachi, who wore a collar of gold, was from Moore's Irish Melodies. But it is difficult to protect the young and it was a cautionary tale for children which set me wandering.

A.E. tells us, in *Song and its Fountains*, that each of us has a governing myth. We discover it in our earliest years and it dominates us even though we have lost all memory of it. In my case it may have been that parable for children which caused me to seek its likeness in the elopement tales of early Gaelic literature and find in them a version of the Platonic ideal. I forgot all about that story until I came across it again by chance when I was assistant editor of a London magazine, the *Argosy*, a position which I held only for a few months because I could not endure captivity in an office in summer. Turning the pages of numbers of the *Strand Magazine* which had appeared in the Nineties, I suddenly saw an illustration of two children vaulting through the air at an unusual height as they chased a rubber ball across Ludgate Circus. I looked down from the high office window at the Circus and remembered that story which I had read so long ago. The little boy and the girl from next door had longed to escape from the suburb in which they lived. One day they chanced on a magic ball and when it bounced over the garden wall they found themselves bounding halfway through the air as they pursued it along the suburbs, across London and beyond. Soon they were alone by themselves at the seaside, bathing, playing on the strand, happy as the day was long. Theirs was all the delight which Adam and Eve had never known. Unfortunately, despite inward warning of what would happen if they did not behave themselves, the little splashers had a tiff one day and immediately the shore grass was hidden by a mile-long promenade. The next time they sulked with one another, a pier with a bandstand was there. To make a short story even shorter, with every quarrel, terraces and hotels spread along the sea front, empty, silent, reproachful. Finally the unhappy children saw the sudden personification of law and order, a policeman keeping his solitary beat on the promenade. The story, as far as I can remember its details, seems to me to have been complex, though it belonged to the pre-Freudian era. Was the writer mocking, consciously or not, the heavy Victorian morality of his time? Did he feel oppressed by the rapid spread of a suburban civilisation?

At any rate his little story has encompassed me because it is still coming true. The old house in which we live at Templeogue Bridge in the deepening shade of trees has been rapidly surrounded by a new suburb and often I think of my first and last visit to James Stephens at Wembley. On a winter's evening, at darkfall, I left the bus stop and walked several miles to Blackbird Farm and found, after much difficulty, the bungalow in which he lived. The handle of the new gate was so stiff that I could not stir it but the gate itself was low and I stepped over it, wondering whether the diminutive poet hopped over it whenever he went in or out. Many years later, when I came to visit him for the last time, the bus stopped in the middle of a crowded shopping centre and I spent half an hour wandering among avenues, crescents and drives before I found the same little bungalow. Often when I venture out in our neighbourhood, I think that I am back again in a suburb of Greater London. Happily there are differences. I pass by more perambulators here, for instance, and yet, despite myself, I cannot help thinking of the Union Jack whenever I glance up and see, proudly displayed in the bedroom windows of many of the recently built villas, our little Penates in red, white and blue. But the names on the gates are not as English as they used to be in Rathmines and Rathgar. The house opposite ours is called Tigh Marian; next to us is Villa Marie, and on the other side is what seems to be a variant, Ladywell.

Twelve

I

SOME months after I had ventured down Capel Street, I decided to revisit more of that neighbourhood on the north side of Dublin which I had avoided for so many years. I chose the hour after lighting-up time for the past is always nearer to us in the decency of darkness. Coming towards O'Connell Bridge, I glanced down a side street and saw an illuminated statue of the Madonna above the doorway of a church-furnishing shop. As the window was as brightly lit, I could not resist the temptation of going down to see the latest in it. While I was looking, I heard the loud strains of jazz music in the shadowy laneway around the corner. I knew that lane well for I had often passed through it on my way to the next one beside the quays where there used to be a long row of secondhand book barrows. There I had met Seumas O'Sullivan for the first time as he searched for rare first editions among the sixpenny, threepenny and penny lots. Every Saturday, book-lovers, poets and students were rummaging through the eighteenth and nineteenth centuries. But my old friend, Joe Pearsadat, whom I had known from childhood when he lived in Upper Dominick Street near us, and all the other vendors and their wares are long since gone. I noticed that there was a small new factory on the left, in which the craftsmen were working overtime for I could hear the sounds of rasping, filing, whirr of belting. Along the shelves of the upper windows were brass vessels, monstrances and chalices which had not yet been gilded. Above the lesser sounds of tool and lathe came the triumphant blare of jazz. The craftsmen had music as they worked.

Hurrying away, I came to Bachelor's Walk and, as I passed by the long patient queues outside the cinemas in O'Connell Street, I remembered the years of British rule, when the infantry men in their smart red jackets and dark blue trousers strolled up and down, silver-knobbed, swagger cane tucked under arm, chatting with innumerable girls or bantering them in noisy groups. In those student years I raged secretly against them for I could not emulate their impudence and taking ways. As I edged by that vanished crowd of Atkinses, the Past poked an elbow in my ribs. Before either of us had time to say excuse me' or 'my fault', I was talking to Frank Meagher. We had just come to the Parnell Monument when he stopped and began to chuckle. I was surprised for he was a student at Maynooth and of a serious disposition. We were both of the same age and, although he was my best friend, I felt jealous of him because he had access to much forbidden knowledge. He was attending lectures in moral theology at that time and the particular subject was what is known as the Sixth and Ninth. Although he was discreet, I could not help feeling that he had an unfair advantage over me and I resented my own lay ignorance. On this occasion, being in holiday mood, he forgot his discretion and shared his amusement with me.

'One of the priests from the Pro-Cathedral was down at the college on a visit recently and told us about a funny experience of his. He was hearing the confession of a young labourer, a big clumsy fellow from one of the tenements in or around Gloucester Street. He had been with a girl a few nights before in a hallway and the priest was questioning him in detail to find out the seriousness of his offence against Holy Purity.

"What did you say she held?"

The labourer lowered his voice modestly. "Me parnell, Father."

"Your what?" exclaimed the puzzled confessor.

"Me parnell, Father".'

'What did he mean?' I was equally puzzled.

So Frank explained to me his theory that in the poorer districts some obscure instinctive memory of ancient priapic cults might have been stirred by that obelisk which the American sculptor, St. Gaudens, had designed. For many years controversy over the adultery of our Protestant leader had divided the country, the Irish Party at Westminster, and all England. Hence the local euphemism.

Such indecent thoughts left me as soon as I had turned the corner. The chemist shop, over which old Mr. O'Duffy, the dentist, had his consulting rooms, seemed unchanged. As I went up the far side of Parnell Square, I met no one. Coming towards Granby Place, I thought of Matt Talbot, the labouring man, who had been found dead outside a stable door in the nearby laneway, with cart chains hidden around his body. I wondered whether I had ever passed him in my boyhood as I made my way down Granby Row to Dominick Street Church. The poor had placed a simple shrine outside the stable and I decided to see if it was still there. As I came to the public house at the corner, I remembered the two boys crouching in the doorway that night when I had seen the three Auxiliaries striding in the middle of the road towards us. But the next moment I forgot that dire encounter for, to my astonishnient, a loud burst of jazz from the laneway assailed me. I looked round the corner and there, in a blaze of light, was the entrance of a new dance-hall and, standing in it, was a commissionaire with peaked hat and pale blue uniform. I went through that unexpected dazzle and, in the shadows a few doors down, the shrine at which passers-by said a few prayers, was still there. The priedieu, the old deal table, much spotted by dust and rain, the couple of cheap vases with withering flowers, all was so simple and affecting that I was deeply moved despite the distracting blare from the dance-hall. I thought of an evening when my mother could not find her spectacles and I read out for her a few chapters from the biography of Matt Talbot which had just been published. It was written by Sir Joseph Glynn, a country solicitor, who had come to Dublin and prospered. He was a loyal servant of the Crown and had been given an important post by a very famous solicitor, Lloyd George. Sir Joseph was well known for his piety and he had gathered patiently in the poorer neighbourhood around Gardiner Street all that was remembered about Matt Talbot. This labouring man had given up daily work, lived on public relief and devoted himself to contemplation and austere practices. As I was reading from the book, I came to a passage in which Sir Joseph was giving examples of Matt Talbot's abstinence. He used to get his sister to boil a fish for him but instead of eating the fish, he gave it to her and humbly drank the water in which it had been boiled.

'But the soup is the most nourishing part of the fish!' exclaimed my mother, and she was so indignant at the selfishness of the saint that she bade me read no more.

Some time before I visited this shrine, clergy and important citizens had been present at a midnight exhumation in order to discover whether the remains of Matt Talbot were miraculously preserved, but there has been no public report of what they witnessed. There are thousands of silent martyrs to rheumatism and horrible diseases; few can escape suffering, yet we marvel at the self-infliction of pain or discomfort. Since the nineteenth century, we have had a succession of great religious organizers, but the popular craving for asceticism still lingers on. The prefect of studies during my last years at school experimented in strange austerities, much to the embarrassment of the Jesuit Order and so none of us knew about it at the time. I thought of Mother Mary Aikenhead, chosen to be foundress of the Sisters of Charity, the daughter of a Scottish Presbyterian doctor who had settled in Cork, and obviously a practical sensible woman. On her death-bed, she asked that an object wrapped in brown paper should be burned in the kitchen range of the convent and many believed that it was a discipline. Suddenly the preposterous vision of a large, middle-aged woman trying to skelp herself at midnight without disturbing the community aroused inner mirth and, remembering how I had told George Moore about it, I was ashamed of myself and turned hastily away. I had not noticed that, on the other side of the lane, opposite to the shrine, was a new repository. When I went over to the window it was too dark for me to see distinctly the little statues, pictures and pamphlets. There was a further surprise. Down the lane was a reddish glow near the railings of the Priory and apse of the church. For a moment it brought back to me those terrors of Hell which I had felt as I went down this lane long ago to confession with my burden of sins. Reflecting the fiery glow was a *Rosary* placard on the Priory railings with the startling announcement: GOD IN LOURDES. Somewhat relieved by this statement, I saw that the infernal glow was only a red bulb over the locked doorway of another new building. It was the Matt Talbot Hall and, on the door was a brass plate with the usual word, 'Offerings'. Pointing down from the high wall beside the building was a cheval-de-frise of long iron spikes, elegant, and yet formidable, for the mendicant orders have always known that there are many ruffians among the poor. That red glow reminded me that the Dominicans were the first inquisitors and had been zealous to obey the divine metaphor: 'If a man abide not in Me he is cast forth as a branch men gather and cast into the fire and they are burned.' The great Continental orders had been brought over by the Norman conquerors and had set up their abbeys next to tower and peel. I hurried past the shrine and the dance-hall again, determined to forget our history, but had hardly got to Granby Row when I saw once more the Bethesda Church which had become a cinema when I was a schoolboy. I knew, of course, that the wicked Cromwell and his troopers stabled their horses in our churches in order to defile and desecrate them. So, I was vaguely surprised when I saw the picture posters for the first time on the pillars outside that church but, like everyone else, accepted the fact and hurried in joyfully with my few pence. Today many Protestant churches here, owing to the decline in the number of parishioners, have become dance-halls and there is merriment in those places where once the Son of Man was worshipped. I find it strange that the sellers do not insist upon some protective clause. Recently, as I drove with a friend at night, past the old British barracks at Droicead Nua, which was taken over by our Government, I saw the leaden panes of the garrison church lit up and thought that the Protestants had come back again but when we came nearer, we heard saxophone and drum.

II

St Mary's Place was echoless and shadowy. The gas lamps had been replaced by electric standards but the light from them was no better than when we ran round the Black Church twice, fearful to do so a third time lest we should see the Devil.

I leaned against the railings of the old Victorian Church and was back immediately in those years at the beginning of this century when I hurried to early Mass on a week day. The eastern light came up from Rutland Square in a dazzle as I hurried past gratings and areas. In the clear air I could sniff the odour of paraffin and, though most of the window blinds were drawn, I knew that women were lighting their kitchen fires. Rattling by on the cobble stones went the Lucan Dairy milk cart, painted yellow, with large nickel can, the driver standing up like a Roman charioteer as he urged his pony. Here and there, as I went down Dorset Street or the short-cut through Granby Lane, I caught up with a few Mass-goers.

I went always to St. Saviour's instead of Berkeley Road Church because I liked the white robes of the Dominicans. When the Secular priests said Mass, I was distracted from my prayers by the glimpses of their black trousers and boots under the hem of the richly coloured vestments, and it was even worse at Benediction, when the officiant climbed the small step-ladder to reach for the Monstrance. I have often wondered why it has not occurred to the clergy to wear a long inner garment and a pair of embroidered mules. There would be the extra trouble of taking off their trousers and boots but the effect would be less incongruous. The church seemed vast and the early light coming through the stained-glass of the orioles and the great rose window added to its mystery, and I always knelt beside one of the pillars although it made me feel smaller than I was. I knew as little of the centuries which passed by us in those twenty minutes as the other worshippers kneeling here and there in the nave and the aisles.

On holy days of obligation I knew an added excitement for there were a number of Masses going on at the same time at the different side-altars, small congregations at each of them, the sound of Latin in the aisles, altar flowers and altar lights wherever I turned. Some people were standing up for the Gospel, others knelt with bowed heads as the bell rang for the Elevation; Masses ended or began, priests and altar boys swept past, people were coming and going. All gave me a sense of multiplicity and of sameness and yet an obscure feeling that there was something irreverent in this simultaneous celebration of the Holy Sacrifice. Years later all came back to me when I read those lines of Rimbaud which seemed to come from a feverish dream of his childhood: '*Madame établit un piano dans les Alpes. La messe et les premières communions se célébrèrent aux cent mille autels de la cathédrale.*'

Such were the religious joys of my childhood but soon I was to be aware of the sorrows. At seven I made my first confession. I cannot remember how and when I was prepared for the sacrament of penance. No doubt I conned the penny catechism in class and learned the sixth commandment, which forbids all looks, words and actions against the virtue of chastity, speech with bad companions, improper dances, immodest company keeping and indecent conversation. In eager anticipation I set forth, proud of having now attained to the theological age of reason and in awe, knowing that the confessor was the visible representative of Christ. I went up Mountjoy Street that morning on our side of the street, past the

Protestant orphanage, Wellington Street corner, and glanced up at the big clock over the public house.

In Berkeley Road chapel, I read the name of Father O'Callaghan over a confessional and, kneeling down, waited till the last penitents had left. Then I opened the side door on the left of the confessional and found myself in the narrow dark recess and, in a minute, the panel was drawn back. I told my little tale of fibs, disobedience and loss of temper and then Father O'Callaghan bent towards the grille and asked me a strange question which puzzled me for I could not understand it. He repeated the question and as I was still puzzled he proceeded to explain in detail and I was disturbed by a sense of evil. I denied everything but he did not believe me and, as I glanced up at the grille, his great hook-nose and fierce eyes filled me with fear. Suddenly the panel closed and I heard Father O'Callaghan coming out of the confession box. He opened the side door and told me to follow him to the vestry. I did so, bewildered by what was happening. He sat down, told me to kneel and once more repeated over and over his strange question, asking me if I had ever made myself weak. The examination seemed to take hours though it must have been only a few minutes. At last, in fear and desperation, I admitted to the unknown sin. I left the church, feeling that I had told a lie in my first confession and returned home in tears but, with the instinct of childhood, said nothing about it to my mother.

It is regrettable that theologians should have brought in this custom of confession at so early an age, when nature itself is endeavouring to protect the growth of personal consciousness. The curiosity and self-display of the infantile phase being quickly forgotten, a child becomes modest, reserved. At the time I was none the worse for my peculiar experience and it was not until later that the effects of this tampering reached too far within me. I can remember very well the special class in which we were instructed when we were about to make our First Communion. The meaning of transubstantiation was beyond our wits but we knew that the sacrament would bring us wonderful joy. Nevertheless I can recollect my disappointment when I became vaguely aware for the first time of ecclesiastical casuistry. We were told we were to receive the Body and Blood of Christ under the appearance of bread and wine. Childlike, I thought of wine as something strange and wonderful and I found it hard to understand why we would not be given the chalice. 'You cannot have a body without blood,' explained Father Gill, 'and therefore if you partake of one species, you share in the other.' I felt puzzled in the same way on another occasion a few years later when another Jesuit was explaining to us in class the nature of the vow of poverty. He took out an expensive gold hunter watch and we all admired it as he pressed something and the lid flew open. 'It's not mine,' said Father Quinlan humbly, 'it belongs to the community.' Yet that treasure was in his vest pocket to be taken out, to be handled, to be delighted in. I think that all the youngsters in the class felt that there was as clever a catch in his words as in the jewelled works of the watch itself.

Of all we were told in our First Communion class, the story of Napoleon impressed us most. We knew, of course, that the Emperor had been punished for his ill-treatment of the Pope. In his last years of exile at St. Helena, someone asked him what had been the happiest day of his life. Instead of mentioning any of his famous victories, he replied simply, 'The day I made my First Communion.' Our own joy was commensurate. I had a new shop suit at last like all the other communicants, with a white silk rosette pinned on the lapel, and we thronged from the chapel to the festive Communion breakfast. My own particular joy and possession was a beautiful prayer book bound in Morocco leather and I clasped it to my breast, ignorant of the Mohamedan hands through which its fine mottling had passed. There were leaflets in it with special prayers and indulgences. Best of all a holy picture of Christ holding a Host above the cup, thus showing that one species was sufficient. Nowadays a rustic custom has spread throughout Dublin and the young have an added reward for their goodness. Little boys in their Communion suits and little girls in their white dresses and veils are brought round to relatives and friends on the happiest day of their lives to collect gifts of half a crown or even five shillings.

III

Every Sunday I went to the altar with my parents. The ceremony being public, I suffered from scruples for I was too conscious at times of my own goodness. I joined hands, lowered eyelids, guided my steps slowly down the aisle again.

I was awed and somewhat frightened by the mystery of impanation, although it was delicate and ethereal. I did not know that the refining of the rite was modern. In the ages of faith, the sacrament was more materialistic. *Frango, panis* – the very sound of the Latin phrase echoes the breaking of the Body on the Cross. In those far-off times, when the senses were cruder, the pious brought their own loaves which were placed at the side of the altar to be transubstantiated. The communicants did not hold a linen cloth under their chins or put out tongue to receive a wafer as we did. Men took the bread in their hands, broke and ate it in lumps. The women, wearing a domino or head cloth, did the same. Then all sipped the Precious Blood through a fistula, and it was not until later centuries that the custom of kneeling was introduced. In the Protestant form of communion, that simple rite survives. Wine is given and, I am told, small cubes of bread. The delicacy and ethereality of our own rite added to its mysteryy to us in childhood when the senses are so sensitive. Indeed when I first saw an advertisement for altar bread in an American religious trade paper, I winced. In Ireland we are still reticent in our approach towards the mysteries and the necessary preparations are hidden from the common eye. The wafers of unleavened bread are lightly cooked and stamped in convents by, if I mistake not, the Sisters of the Good Shepherd. In piles like coins, they are parcelled and despatched by post to our city churches every week. Unused or stale wafers are reserved for the Dry Mass, the six months rehearsal which students have before ordination.

IV

There was a strict rule at home that I must go to Confession every Saturday in order to receive Holy Communion next morning. I did so with much seriousness and was puzzled by what I regarded as the levity of my sisters. Gaily, they hurried down to their favourite confessor, Father Marrett. He was a handsome man, a popular preacher, and there was always a row of young girls outside his confessional. He kept the lattice curtains wide open and was accustomed to chat to those young sinners after they had been absolved. As I passed, I was always shocked to see his tonsured head inclined to left or right, his lips moving, not in prayer but in trivial talk. On one occasion, after he had given her absolution, he said as usual to Kathleen.

'And how is my little pet this week?'

'I'm not your little pet any more. I have just heard you telling Josie Tierney that she is your pet now.'

As Father Marrett had spoken loudly, she had overheard him though the shutter was closed and, in her indignation, she forgot that she was committing the grave sin of jealousy.

Father Marrett's eye roved while he was confessing or chatting. Once, at the font near the doorway, an eccentric, shabbily- dressed woman pushed rudely against my sister and, when she protested, flung a handful of holy water in her face. Instantly Father Marrett bounded from his confession box but when he got to the swinging baize door the sacrilegist had fled. Eventually this happy-hearted Son of St. Dominic yielded to the pleasures of drink. He took to visiting the hospitable houses in the neighbourhood. Indeed the thirsty monk arrived so often on our doorstep that my mother had to hide the decanter.

My own Father Confessor sat in the next box. He was young, gentle, pale-laced, very emotional. Father O'Hara listened, questioned me sadly and then repeated a little homily on the sufferings which Jesus had endured all for my sake. After the absolution, he gave me only a few Hail Marys as a penance. Sometimes I felt ashamed to go to him because I fancied he must know my little budget of sins by heart for I never seemed to improve. There were always the same venial faults: I had spoken in an uncharitable way to one of my sisters, lost my temper, was a few minutes late for Mass, did not obey my parents at once. But all was to culminate soon in an explosion of fear and shame. One Saturday evening I had come home from confession and lost my temper in some dispute within a minute or two. 'Damn you!' I shouted at my mother. I knew by the heat in my face and the terrible strange tone in my voice that the Devil had taken instant possession of me. My poor mother was equally convinced and, as she told me, saw my soul burning in hell. Fearful that I might drop down in that state of sin, she hurried me back to confession at once. Along Dorset Street that winter's evening I struggled, overwhelmed with horror of myself and conscious that, from the sky, the angered Man Above, to use my father's constant phrase, was watching me. One moment, I was Cain fleeing through the wilderness; the next, I was the Boy Who had Cursed His Own Mother. Already I was passing between walls of flame that hid the provision shops, the Fire-brigade Station, the house opposite, in which Richard Brinsley Sheridan had lived and the high railings of the Priory. In my mind's eye I could see the collecting card of the Third Order of Franciscans which had so often chilled me – an arm raised from the fiery pit clad not in samite but in asbestos. It was not the flames of Purgatory but those of Hell itself which threatened me and I could hear their dull roar. I made the sign of the cross at the font as I dashed into the church for I knew that in a few minutes more all the priests would have left. My only chance was Father O'Hara. He had confessed me only a short time before but his meekness and gentleness would save me again. I was just in time and I trembled as I awaited the familiar question.

'How long is it, my child, since your last confession?'

'Twenty minutes, Father.'

Perhaps he did not quite hear my mumbled explanation, perhaps he was weary. Certainly he showed no sign of consternation when I mentioned my dreadful offence against the third commandment. Once more he repeated the little homily on the sufferings which Jesus had endured for my sake. I scarcely listened to those sentiments which I knew so well for, wild with superstition, I only wanted to hear the unintelligible words in Latin for they alone could save me. To my own astonishinent, my dread and mental pain completely disappeared as soon as I left the church. Happily I tripped past provision shops, the Fire-brigade Station, ran past the Black Church in St. Mary's Place. Once more I was a good boy.

V

That experience, however, was but the beginning of many as I came to the age of puberty and the promptings of the Devil increased. I heard in the school chapel the celebrated sermon on Hell which James Joyce has described. Constantly I listened for the ticking of the great clock below. Religious instruction and retreats made us all aware of the millions of human beings condemned to eternal torture. We gazed at mournful holy pictures of martyrdom on earth, of hangings, choppings and burnings. We were told exemplary stories of sinners on their deathbeds surrounded by demons, waiting to snatch their souls, finding so enormous a last breath that they could be heard throughout the neighbourhood screeching for a priest to save them. We prayed daily for a happy death and our thoughts were mortuary. Fear of eternal torture is historic with us and traditional jokes signify its intensity. Driven back, that fear returns in middle age and our remedies against it are desperate. So, for instance, a Cork industrialist, who delighted to watch bathing belles in his illuminated swimming pool, gave his city a large church, which must have cost a fortune. Locally it is still known as O'Dwyer's Fire-Escape.

Ignorant and confused by physical development and the change in scrotal sensation, I became convinced that the Devil entirely possessed me and, startled by the first bristles below, I seized a scissors and in an agony of alarm shore myself. In class we heard much about the temptations against which the saints had struggled – Augustine, Francis Xavier, Gonzaga. How could we escape? Alphonsus de Ligouri had been sustained for many years by heavenly visions. On one occasion a ray of divine light darted towards him, as he was preaching, from a picture of Our Lady. He had been levitated and at times he was in more places than one for he had the miraculous power of bi-location. Nevertheless, three years before his death, when he was eighty-nine, he entered into that dark night of the soul which we knew already in our teens. Fearful temptations assailed him day and night; the Devil conjured up unchaste sights before him.

Equally puzzling to a young mind was the mixture of ferocity and fervour in religion. While we were struggling against our base instincts, we were yielding to the voluptuous language of the Spanish and French mystics. In the chill language of English, these prayers of the baroque period were excessive since the young are reserved and shy. I was used to the discipline of music, severe scales and exercises. I knew that I must not vibrate the strings too much and that continual tremulo was in bad taste. Popular tunes that the messenger boys whistled as they passed by constantly tempted me, but I felt better again when the small German band, which came to our street once a week, played waltzes. The old man and his four sons were excellent musicians and I knew they could not be mistaken in their choice.

When I was on my knees, however, I was embarrassed by those exclamatory prayers, perfumed as incense, sharp as the red hot charcoals. My mother had been embarrassed by an angel's prayer; I was afflicted by the continual litanies in my teens: *O Most adorable, precious and infinitely tender Heart pierced for the love of me, pierce my heart with the love of Thee.* Such words drew me down to unknown depths. *Sacred Heart, I put my trust in Thee. Inflame my heart with Thy love. O Wisdom of the Sacred Heart! O light of the Sacred Countenance, shine upon us. O Love of the Sacred Heart, consume me in Thy fire.* These aspirations, oft repeated, were so powerful that they could save us from a hundred days purgatory, even give us remission of seven years from the flames.

Soon compulsory confession was to become a weekly ordeal. Obscurely, through the grille, came warnings against curiosity, body-blighting sins, voluntary emissions that would eventually bring on madness. The Devil was at my side, tempting with his sweets of darkness, urging me to cunning evasive devices. Whenever I had offended against the sixth commandment, I endeavoured to slip in this mortal sin between venial ones, and it was difficult because I kept most of the other commandments. I was rarely disobedient for I did not like my ears boxed; I was by nature truthful, seldom late for Mass. So I had to persuade my conscience and exaggerate moments of distraction when praying or inattention when the priest was in the pulpit. Often I succeeded in my cunning but at times I failed and was closely examined for particulars. I was matching my wits against the centuries. Whenever I saw a large number of penitents outside a confessional, I suspected that the priest was not strict and, to make certain, I waited patiently until almost the last to make sure that he was feeling tired. For some time after I became ashamed to confess my sins to Father O'Hara, I discovered by chance that Father Gough, though gruff in his manner, was very hard of hearing. One Saturday, I had an unusually large burden of bad thoughts: being truthful, I had tried to count them as they flitted in and out of my mind. The choleric old man must have caught my faint whisper he exclaimed. 'How many times did you say?' 'Forty times, Father.' 'Get out of me box, yeh young blaggard.' I crept out, shamefaced, fearing that the other penitents had heard his angry words. It was getting late and I was faced once more with the problem of returning home in a state of grace. There was only one hope left on earth – the gentle Father O'Hara who knew so well all the sufferings of the young. I hurried over to the 'Poor Side' of the chapel, passed the Figure of the Crucifix, the nailed feet black with the kisses of the people. There was always on the Poor Side a heavy smell like that which came from the hallways of the tenements in Dorset Street, but it comforted me now in my spiritual squalor. I was the last sinner and Father O'Hara had already taken off his stole. He put it on again, listened patiently to my confused explanation. 'Did you take pleasure in these thoughts?' 'Yes, Father.' 'Did you . . .' He hesitated and his voice was almost a sigh. 'Did you let your nature flow?' 'No, Father.' I heard once more the sound of the soul-washing Latin and I hurried homeward, safe for a few more days from the torments of the world below.

My moral degradation rapidly increased. Soon I was roaming through the slums to distant churches for I felt that among the horrible sins confessed in them by the 'lower orders', mine would scarcely be noticed. In secret, I envied my sisters who were untroubled and went so happily to confession every week and whenever I heard them talking of a popular priest or of a new one, I ventured to his box. Sometimes, in sullen mood, I tried to console myself with cases of irreverence among the clergy. I thought of two city priests known as Thunder and Lightning, for one was so slow and ponderous at the altar that all but the very pious avoided his Mass. The other gabbled so quickly that his 'short twelve' on Sunday was thronged.

When we had moved to another house on the north side, I discovered Father Carroll and Father Geoghegan, both of whom were eccentric. Every Saturday morning all the children from the National School nearby came to be confessed and the two elderly clergymen spent much time trying to dodge their duty. Sometimes Father Carroll delayed as long as he could and his unfortunate rival was left to deal with the scores of little prattlers. He sent children in relays to the presbytery opposite with urgent messages for Father Carroll to come over, and the following Saturday, Father Geoghegan would go on strike and Father Carroll would send the youngsters for him. Father Carroll, unlike his spiritual opponent, was tall, aristocratic and proud of his descent. I knew him well for he came frequently to our house though he was never invited. He had artistic tastes and, whenever he liked an ornament on the mantelpiece, a vase or even a fine old chair or picture which my mother had bought at the auction rooms, he asked for it. Everywhere he went, he asked, and, as he was seldom refused, he had a large collection of bric-a-brac. Eventually his mania became so bad that he was sent to a remote glen in Co. Wicklow, where his parishioners possessed only pot-hooks, skillets and three-legged stools.

Owing to my iniquity, Sunday morning became to me almost hallucinatory, so many were the distractions with which the Devil afflicted me. Like Guido Reni and his fellow painters, I snatched away the loin cloth from the crucifix. I was seized by the speculative curiosity of Aquinas. In my ignorance, I was aware of the stercorarian heresies of medieval thinkers. Even in the very midst of communion I was no longer safe: eye quick as mind, was always being distracted. I glimpsed the coming chalice with its pile of consecrated wafers, was aware of the scent of soap on the celebrant's hand as it passed and of the tongues protruded beside me. 'Hypocrite, hypocrite!' murmured the Evil One as I left the rail, my eyelids lowered while I watched the slippery marble steps and the floor tiles. I murmured prayers vainly but my love was false and all my feelings were cold. I feared the particle against my palate; despite my reverence, I was aware of the hollows in my decaying teeth, the spittle in my gullet. Doubts of myself assailed me, for, as a result of my trickery and deception, I had come to the conclusion that all my confessions, one after another, were bad. The suspicions of my spiritual state deepened. Had I made fifty bad confessions and communions in a year or not? If so, week after week, the damning figures were mounting. Too well I remembered those terrible tales of the *Hosties Sanglantes*. In particular there was the story of a wicked Jew who doubted the truth of transubstantiation and decided to make a test. Often at night I watched that frenzied old man glaring with hate as he drove a bread knife into the Host in a workshop or cellar. I saw the drops and then the miraculous torrent of the Holy Blood which poured around him. There was another story which was as fearful. My tongue would blacken: I would be struck dead as I left the rails and my poor father and mother would see their wretched offspring expiring horribly, his shame and theirs exposed before all the congregation as his filthy soul was borne off by the Devil.

The mental pains of the young are intermittent for there is so much to discover. Slowly and surely I emerged from the Counter Reformation though, whenever I glanced over my shoulder, I could see its cassocked figures in the transept or smiling on the steps of the gymnasium. It was not, however, until I was twenty-three that I found out in Paris that the machinations of the Devil had been, in my case, made easier by a slight physical defect. A young woman who was giving me a course in French conversation told me so. '*Il faut couper le filet,*' she said and sent me off to a surgeon. He gave me a local anaesthetic and the operation was a simple one for the scissoring took only a couple of minutes. Putting his hand on my shoulder, he explained why he had spared me the last snip. Although I was feeling faint at the time I have never forgotten his kindly words.

'*Mon enfant, vous aurez plus de platisir comme çal!*'

Thirteen

I

'THE nearer the church, the farther from God.' So runs the proverb and, by an inscrutable set of circumstances, I spent most of my early life within stone's throw of some church or another. When my mother took a house in Co. Dublin near Killiney, we were next door to the presbytery and, from the back room in which I wrote, I could see, between the trees, at night, the dimly illumined stained-glass windows of the church and hear the murmur of devotions. Every weekday at half a minute to twelve o'clock, came the voices of schoolboys running helpfully to swing the bellrope, and at nine-thirty in the evening, the last sounds were those of the chapel clerk locking the doors and shuffling down the gravel path to his home. There was one other sound to which I owe much. Only a wall divided my bedroom from that of the junior curate in the presbytery. With unfailing regularity, I heard, at midnight, despite the thickness of the wall, two rustic crashes in rapid succession as he rid himself of his boots. One night I lay listening to the dreamiest sound in the world, the sound of our soft Irish rain in the trees between my window and the locked church. I was awaiting also the two bumps. For some months I had been thinking over our forgotten medieval Ireland when we almost had a religion of our own and had been searching for some image which would bring me other images. Midnight came but there was silence in that room next to mine and I remembered at last that the curate had gone away on his annual visit to the Continent. In that inner silence, the image for which I had been groping came into my mind:

> Rainfall
> Was quiet as the turning of books
> In the holy schools at dawn.

Although I do not live at present within earshot of a church, I am almost within view of seminaries which are rapidly increasing, in number and extent. 'In the south are the people of Christ' runs an old Gaelic saying and in the south-east, a few points out of reckoning, is a large Jesuit seminary. Every evening the rooks in a flock pass our house on their way back from the last dairy farms to the beeches surrounding the Castle in which the students live. I have but to close my eyes and see that ornamental pond in which the prefect of our school used to immerse himself secretly on winter nights until the castellan happened to look out and mistook him for a non-Catholic ghost of the eighteenth century. On the west, near the legendary plague-pits of Parthalon, is a Dominican seminary which greatly influenced my life. For here, as a city child, on a Sunday outing, I saw for the first time, under the ancient trees in the demesne, a patch of bluebells. I saw them for a few seconds as I hurried with my father towards the gateway for we were almost late for the steam-tram. But those seconds were unforgettable. Years afterwards, when I started a poem about Diarmuid and Grainne, the first lines I wrote came from my glimpse of what was under those gloomy trees.

On the north-east, immediately across the road, is the postern to another seminary almost a mile away, belonging to a missionary order, whose very name would fascinate any poet — the Fathers of the Holy Ghost. Looking from my bedroom window towards the Dublin Hills, I can see Mount Venus, where George Moore and his imaginary mistress were wont to be. The eighteenth century house in which he lived for a time is now a ruin but above the next slope of fields there is an Augustinian noviciate: the father-house of an enormous new seminary which has just been completed little more than a mile away at Ballyboden. Until recently we used to buy fresh eggs from the old woman in the gate lodge of Templeogue House for she had about twenty good layers. Charles Lever, the well-known novelist, lived there once and was lavish in his hospitality. Often at the gate, I thought of Thackeray and others who had been entertained in that house. But when I came one day to buy a dozen new-laids, the lodge was empty and there was a decorators' board on the gate. The Maynooth Mission to China, undeterred by persecution in the Communistic East, had acquired the estate for a third seminary. A few weeks later I happened to meet an old neighbour who lives in one of the cottages near the estate and we chatted in verse, a custom that still lingers, here and there, within the Pale.

> 'I see you've got new landlords! How do you like
> Them?'
> 'Very well. Last week they let us have
> Some apples.'
> 'Where has Mr. White gone?'
> 'Somewhere
> Near Monkstown.'
> 'I hear they paid him ten thousands pounds.'
> 'That's right and, by the look o' things, they'll spend
> As much on alterations and improvements:
> And nearly everyone with his own car.
> Where *do*, they get the money, Mr. Clarke?'
> 'From us.'
> 'They don't get much from me. Indeed
> It's hard enough to pay the rent itself.
> But there, I mustn't complain: the health's good and soon
> We won't have far to go to Mass on Sundays!'

Sometimes when I feel ungratefully that we are all being encircled by a monstrous regimen of celibacy, I lower my eyelids and, in spirit, frequent again the streets and byways of London. I hurry towards Fleet Street and the pre-Reformation era dwindles to a few scattered names: Covent Garden, Carmelite House, Blackfriars. At a dingy corner under the railway bridge near Printing House Square there is a tavern with a brightly coloured frieze depicting corpulent jolly monks, tankards in hand, around their refectory board. It was the early work of a well-known R.A., and, when I first saw it, I did not dream that I was destined to fall in love with his young wife. Indeed I stared at the revelling monklings with patriotic indignation, regarding the frieze as a typical example of Protestant contempt and superficiality. I forgot for the nonce that I had written a poetic comedy based on the story of Anier Mac Conglinne, a medieval poet, who satirized the wealthy monks of Corc after a hungry night in their guest-house, where a myriad fleas had fed on his frailty. The Irish Goliard had parodied the liturgy so outrageously both in prose and verse that, for the honour of our country, I did not feel that I could borrow his invective.

Going to and from Fleet Street, I met some who had known the poets of the Victorian age: Mr. Reeves, the elderly bookseller to whom we took our review copies, had often seen William Morris in his father's shop. He still remembered how alarmed he was, as a boy, whenever the poet came in to look at books. He was low-sized, bearded and dressed in an extraordinary fashion of his own for he wore a loose jacket and a bright blue shirt – and he always seemed angry. When I was working for Caradoc Evans and Con O'Leary, who were joint editors of *T.P.'s Weekly*, we adjourned every day during the lunch hour to a wine cellar at Ludgate Circus. The manager, a quiet, elderly little man, told us one day that, when he was a young serving lad there, Oscar Wilde used to come over from La Belle Sauvage where he was editing *Woman's World*. He sat at the counter on one of the high stools and occasionally, when he was paying for drinks, he tucked a half crown in his trouser crease – the side on which he dressed,' explained the manager in his staid manner. Half a crown was a large sum in 1888 and if the youth removed the coin, the Irish poet told him to keep it.

Later when my wife and I were living in Hertfordshire a few miles away from St. Albans, I liked to stray around Romeland with its memories both of the ancient Verulamium and the pre-Reformation era, moving among names and places; Waxhouse Gate, where the monks moulded their ceremonial candles, Abbey Mill Lane, Fishpool Street, Holywell Hill. Herbert Palmer, the poet of dissent, was a well-known figure in the Cathedral city, and sometimes we drank the local beer in the Old Fighting Cocks or, as it was sometimes called, the Old Round House, formerly a monastic fishing lodge. One day, as I was meditating alone beneath the simple memorial at Monastery Gate on the spot where John Tankerford, one of the first reformers, had been burned at the stake on the 26th August 1555, I remembered a remark of my childhood. My mother had been telling me how the wicked Henry VIII had confiscated all the lands and properties of the religious communities. 'But where did they get them all?' I asked innocently.

II

Since the establishment of our republic, many Continental orders have spread again throughout our country. Children of today have for their delight the florality of names such as The Faithful Companions of Jesus, the Handmaidens of the Sacred Heart of Jesus, the Daughters of the Cross, the Sisters of the Cross and Passion, the Blue Sisters, the Poor Servants of the Mother of God, the Daughters of the Heart of Mary, the Sisters of Mary Reparatrix, the Sisters of Marie Auxiliatrix, the Little Sisters of the Assumption, Our Lady of the Cenacle, the Little Company of Mary, the Sisters of Bon Secours, the Sisters of St. Joseph of Chambery, the Sisters of St. Joseph of Cluny. Along our road, almost opposite the Carmelite College, a new order has acquired part of the estate once owned by the wealthy relatives of G. Bernard Shaw. This community has a name which reads like a literal translation from French: The Religious of Education. The sisters wear the wimple with a difference and sometimes, as a young one trips along the pavement, it looks to my wolfish eye like a pretty black riding-hood. This school is expensive and large cars, steered by happy mothers, drive up to fetch home children in neat brown uniforms with embroidered badge. Quickly, as in a fairy tale, a Civic Guard appears at the crossroads, smiling as he directs this temporary traffic.

My first glimpse of those large American cars brought back to me the worldly pangs which I had endured as a youngster at school for they were almost greater than my spiritual woes. The snobbery of our Jesuit College, which was an imitation of a well-known Catholic public school in England, was inescapable. Most of the fathers of my school companions were of the professional classes, doctors, barristers, higher civil servants or else merchants and hotel proprietors. 'What is your father?' was a constant question both in the playground and in the class-room. So I dreaded the day when I would have to admit that mine was only an official in the Corporation. To make matters worse, my father, despite his rapid promotion, had never changed his easy-going ways and was not always as grammatical in his speech as I was. High and low were the same to him and whenever I went out with him for a walk or a cycle run, he was hail-fellow-well-met with everyone. He would stop and talk to scavengers shovelling up horse dung, dustmen emptying bins, call out to roadmen and paviors. He chatted to the water inspectors with their tell-tale uniform, while I waited anxiously lest Father Gill, the aristocratic Father O'Mara, or our mathematics teacher, Father Quinlan might pass by, or, worse still, some of the boys from my own class, for this would mean my lasting disgrace. I had been sent to a superior college because it was the only way to save me from the excessive corporal punishment in schools that cost only fourpence a week. It happened in this way.

When I left the small convent class in Dominick Street, I was sent to the National School in Dorset Street. I spent only two days there and vaguely remember the large crowded playground and the lay teachers. No doubt the grimy urchins there were careless as they played and tumbled about on the dusty ground but, when I came back and innocently reported that all the other children ate black bread, my mother was horrified. No doubt a child who had suffered from gastric fever with all its torments of vertigo and cerebral expansion, a child who had so often to be coaxed back to appetite with arrowroot and sponge cakes sopped in sherry, could not be exposed to the risks of a National School. So on the following Monday I was taken to the Christian Brothers in St. Mary's Place, not more than twenty running steps from the Black Church. The dim memory of the first and only week which I spent there is still Freudian to me, a veritable frenzy of repression and sadistic celibacy. All day in that high hall with its crowded benches, standing and sitting classes, through the din of lessons and sing-song of spellings, came the interminable dread sounds of slappings and beatings. Monitors and even favourites among the boys were allowed to punish the younger children. Every day I was slapped for no reason, like many others, and on Thursday I was put across a bench. The spanking was so light that it might have been in sport but I felt very much the indecency and humiliation. When I came back to the top bench against the wall, a cousin of mine murmured in my ear a popular song which I knew to be very wicked for the chorus went 'Tarara boom-de-ay', and my cousin kept poking me in the ribs as he emphasised the forbidden word in the middle of the refrain — 'tarara boom-de-ay. On Friday the climax came when I told my mother, truthfully, that I had been given fourteen slaps during lessons.

There was much indignation in my home at this unjust treatment and in a fine rage my father rushed round the corner on Saturday morning and told the Brother Superior what he thought of him. I must add that I had always been punished by my parents in the strict Protestant manner of the Victorian age, for the priests of our neighbourhood were under the impression that 'spare the rod and spoil the child' came from the Bible. That text was constantly repeated in our house and my mother would have been filled with consternation if she had been told that it was composed by a seventeenth century English poet.

Some time ago, a league of Dublin parents was formed to protect children from excessive corporal punishment in our schools and this desperate remedy aroused many protests among the elderly. The ex-President of Ireland, Mr. Sean T. O'Kelly declared publicly that the beatings which he got as a pupil in the school at St. Mary's Place had done him a world of good. Perhaps subconsciously those larrupings made a rebel of him and hastened his revolutionary activities against an alien government! My parents did not realize what they were really doing when, doubtlessly, after much counting and thinking of ways and means, they decided to trust me, at the age of seven, to the costly Society of Jesus.

On that fatal morning of enrolment, my mother and I waited in the drawing-room of the college in Gardiner Place. On the ceiling of that eighteenth-century room, all aswirl, were pictured women and chubby urchins with little or nothing on them. However, I had never heard of pagan mythology and it is much easier for the shy to look down than to look up. In came the Rector, very tall and corpulent, holding his biretta which had a big velvety bob in the middle. He glanced at me kindly and yet sharply through his bi-focal glasses. Anxious and yet proud of me, my mother waited as he questioned me. She had already prepared me for the preliminary examination, but she had not realized that the Jesuit order is an intellectual one and always informed about scientific advances. I was surprised, therefore, when the Rector avoided religious subjects and, after chatting with my mother, turned to me.

'Tell me, Austin, what shape is the world?'

'Round, Father, like, like an orange.'

'And does it move?' he prompted.

'Yes, Father, round the sun.'

"*Thou hast conquered, O pale Galileo!*"

III

At my new college I was to hear much about the Christian Brothers, for their pupils gained most of the prizes and exhibitions in the Junior, Middle and Senior grades of the Intermediate Examination. No doubt a sense of rivalry was responsible for this uncharitableness, but the Christian Brothers, whose livelihood was dependent, to some extent, on capitation grants, were crammers and this rightly disturbed the Jesuit Fathers with their long tradition of classical education. All was orderly and punishment, as in my own home, was arranged in a systematic manner to avoid injustice and the danger of lost temper. Those guilty of inattention, talking in class, passing of notes, impudence, carelessness, idleness and other offences were given a note with the number of required slaps written on it. They had to wait in turn at two o'clock at the end of a short flight of wooden steps leading to a loft. There Mr. Black, who was within a few years of his ordination, was waiting to administer impartial punishment. He might have been chosen for his height and vigour; indeed he seemed gigantic because of the low rafters. The instrument of torture, known as a pandebat, was a thick leather strap with thick stitches along the side which could almost have been designed on purpose for, to the numbing effect of the slap, they added extremely painful stinging. Youngsters can comprehend a blow struck in anger, even a good kick, or a well-aimed slipper, but an impersonal system makes them aware of their own helplessness against the brute force of their elders. Unfortunately, in the case of sensitive children, the hours of miserable anticipation increase tenfold the actual punishment. We knew that the torments in the next world were more horrible but such knowledge only added to the gloom of our present existence. I must have felt all deeply for I have never forgotten one day at two o'clock, when the discipline of the centuries was shattered for a moment by the might of kindness. It was in springtime and I had lingered to the last of the queue, listening to the crack of the leather and watching the boys come down, one by one, squeezing or blowing their hands. The corridor was silent, the sunlight shone through the high windows and yet I hesitated to creep up to that abstract monster hidden above. To my horror, the Prefect of Studies suddenly appeared from downstairs. We were all in awe of Father McKenna, although he was absent-minded, because he had bushy eyebrows and even when he was not frowning, seemed to be. We did not know that he was a distinguished Gaelic scholar and had edited many manuscripts.

'What are you doing here?' he exclaimed.

Mutely I showed him the slip of paper with the figure of eight on it. He must have recognized my plight instantly for he pretended not to notice it. He glanced down at me from his bushy eyebrows with a ferocious frown which I understood at once.

'Off with you now to your class or you'll be late.' So, with another mock frown, my fellow conspirator shooed me away.

As James Joyce has recounted his experiences at the same college a generation earlier in his *Portrait of the Artist as a Young Man*, it would be vain of me to attempt to describe similar events during my own time there since little seemed to have changed, except that our English master, Mr. George Dempsey, the only lay teacher employed, had become white-haired and was eating peppermints to relieve his indigestion.

Outside school hours, the young have a private existence of their own. I looked forward every day to my homeward journey for several reasons although it usually spoiled my appetite. Michael, my particular friend, lived in the opposite direction, but he accompanied me most of the way and then took a tram to Drumcondra. His parents owned a fruit-shop in Capel Street and, as he was their only child, he had an enormous supply of pocket money. He bought all the comic papers and, after he had glanced at the picture pages, he handed them to me, for he was too indolent to read the short stories and the serials in diamond print. So as we went home slowly pacing, I re-told the wild, violent and blood-thirsty events to him and he rewarded me with helpings from the bags of sweets bulging in his jacket pockets. When more supplies of liquorice allsorts, creams and Cleeve's toffee were necessary, we stopped at one of the sweet-shops in Granby Place. Adventures were not always sufficient. There was a semi-circle of gravel outside Charlemont House, just beyond Findlater's Church, a constant temptation, which has now been removed. Disgracing our Belvederean caps, we whirled around the semi-circle, dodging around the steps, stooping and flinging handfuls of gravel at each other. One day, as I stooped for a handful, I saw my mother on the far side of Rutland Square. She was low-sized and stout but she always walked with the brisk light step of a girl. Had she seen me, I would have been punished by my father with his strop when he came back from the office in Castle Street. Fortunately I was not seen but I never played that game again.

The reading of all those comic stories involved me in much subterfuge for my time was limited. I kept one on my knee while I was practising my scales, ready to whip it into my pocket or sit on it whenever I heard a step on the stairs. But I paid dearly twice a week for these guilty joys. I attended in Rathmines an Academy of Music which had just been opened by Professor O'Dwyer. He was not only a pianist but a composer and I regarded him with mingled awe and astonishment for he was quite unlike Chopin or Mendelssohn. His grey hair was so closely cropped that it made his small, monkey-like face even smaller. Far different was my violin teacher, Mr. Darley, tall, handsome, with long bony hands. He swayed as his bow heeled or tipped the strings, his eyes half-closed as the crochets and semiquavers multiplied around us and to me he was as mysterious and remote as Paganini. He enriched the ancient Irish airs collected by Bunting and Petrie with double-stopping and I envied him his gift, for the single notes of the violin seemed to me chilling unless accompanied by piano. He was shadowy, impersonal. Yet from the distance, that dear man spoiled me because at the end of each term he said a few encouraging words to me and presented me shyly with a five-shilling box of chocolates. I was quite surprised a few years ago when Dr. T. J. Kiernan, one of our ambassadors, told me that he had been in the same violin class and that all the other youngsters, including himself, had regarded me as a disgusting little prig. Little did those scrapers know what I endured on winter evenings after I had run down the steps of the Music Academy.

There was a long avenue to the house and half-way along it was a double row of trees making the abrupt blackness of a railway tunnel. My problem was to get safely through that place of ambush. As soon as I came to it, demons, witches, the Liverpool ghost, crooks, cut-throats, scalpers, garrotters, and such like criminals from the pages of the Penny Dreadfuls were waiting for me. My greatest woe was an interminable serial which I recounted week after week to Michael as he complacently sucked toffee or acid drops. The age of invention in which we were living was depicted in that story with all its excitement and misuse. A wicked inventor had made a large steel torpedo with whirling blades which could cut its way subterraneously at so great a speed that the law-abiding were no longer safe. The victims of his gang would hear a low rumbling like that of an underground London train. The rumbling became a roar and the basement of a house shook, then through the rending floor boards, the cap of the torpedo lifted, the flanges rang, the metal trap opened and the villains jumped out, brandishing their revolvers. As I fled past many villainous faces, I could hear underneath the field on my left the dull rumble of the engines in the subterranean torpedo. My only hope was to keep looking at the street lights which seemed so far away, watch the illuminations of the passing trams. However, in a minute or two, I was sitting triumphantly, my violin case across my knees, on the top of a tram waiting until we came into glory at O'Connell Bridge. There were four track rows and, as the trams kept passing by, the lights were reflected many times through their glass. During those few minutes of bridge-crossing I fancied that around the passengers was the glitter of their attendant spirit. Curiously enough our belief in guardian angels is complete only when we are very small and schoolboys are as little aware of the invisible companion as adults are. Fearborne down the dark avenue at Rathmines, I never thought of the invisible wings beside me nor did it occur to me that my constant visionary experience while crossing O'Connell Bridge might have been a silent reproach to me for ingratitude.

The young and old are still busied in thought in this age of ever-increasing inventions but much seems reversed. When I was growing up, we were greatly concerned at school with the horrors of the next world, but outside school hours we were excited by the new discoveries which were being made in this world and, despite our spiritual certainties, we were dimly aware of a century of revelation. The name of Edison was a household possession and we were always hearing of his latest inventions. My maternal uncles had all emigrated to the United States long before I was born, but one of them had come back and was a water inspector in my father's office. He had learned to diet in the States and took for breakfast a raw onion in his 'stirabout', and then broke a couple of eggs into his cup of cocoa. When he came home from work, he regaled himself with dandelion tea. In consequence he lived to be well over eighty. Uncle Maurice had brought other interests with him from the New World to keep up his strength and give him pleasure. He had a mysterious contraption which emitted pin-and-needle shocks, and a phonograph with cylindrical records. Electricity was already home-made and I was always present when my father renewed the sal ammoniac in the glass jar of the battery which was used for the hall-door bell. Soon we had electric fittings in the house but the switches, which were made of brass, could often be as painful to the touch as Uncle Maurice's energy-giving machine. One summer, a handsome American woman, who was a distant cousin of ours, came to Dublin on a visit with her little red-ringleted daughter. Melia had brought with her a pair of roller skates and I practised with them on the footpath round the Black Church whenever she lent them to me, wildly clutching the railings. Soon after they returned to America, Melia's mother sent me a pair of skates. I like to think that I was the first skater to appear in the Dublin streets, for I hurried down Capel Street as often as I could to Mary Street, where there was the only stretch of macadam in the city. There I sped between vans and floats, alarming myself and the sparrows that flew up from the fresh horse-droppings. A few years later, the skating craze had spread to Dublin and a large rink was hastily built in the green enclosure of Rutland Square. There, by the hour, we sped among hundreds through the two or three inches of thunder around our footsteps. Not content with this, I clattered, lurched precariously, stumbled and clung in the ringlet reserved for beginners, spreading much alarm; then, showing off in the most disgusting way, I glided back to the main floor. Doto was a skilful skater and a much better waltzer than I was. For the first Fancy Dress Competition held at the Rotunda Rink, she designed a picturesque costume, wreathed late flowers and spent much time sewing on russet leaves. She won a prize as Autumn, for the poetic simplicity of the costume appealed to the judges as much as the ingenuity of the bloated Michelin Tyres and the Ship-wrecked Sailor on the Raft. Later on, another rink was opened at Earlsfort Terrace but it did not last long because of what had happened at a Fancy Dress Ball there. It was rumoured that the Bird, a well-known practical joker, had appeared in a long crimson robe, a false beard and a transformation of auburn ringlets. He was hastily removed and from that night all avoided the accursed place. I heard other stories about this

Edwardian prankster but I was too young to understand their full significance. On one occasion he had driven slowly down Grafton Street with a dummy woman's leg protruding from the cab window. Cabs were often used for immoral purposes and, at night-time, it was not always safe to glance down at one of them from the top of a tram passing along the ill-lighted Merrion Square.

We are so used to the rapidity of motor traffic that it is strange to think of a time when young and old were protected from the danger of speed by stone walls, railings, white gates and red signals. Often, on the way to paddle and pick cockles at Merrion Strand, we waited at the level crossing until the train had passed and even after the rattle and roar were distant we stepped over the sunken rails with considerable caution and anxiety. One day, at the corner of George's Street, at a few yards from Dame Street, I saw for the first time a motor car on the public road. A large, resentful crowd surrounded it and was jeering what remained of the driver, for only his trouser ends and boots could be seen as he lay on his back under the machine tinkering at it. It is possible, too, that I saw the the first child killed by a motor car in this country and I have never forgotten the tragedy of that summer's day. Kathleen and I were in the Phoenix Park on our way to the Wellington Monument, for this manifestation of British rule gave much pleasure to the young. Scores of children were always scrambling up and sliding down the wide steps. As we were passing on the opposite side of the People's Gardens, two boys cycled past, then, a motor car came along at a slow pace. Something happened and one of the boys was lying on the road, his throat mangled, his Norfolk jacket covered with dust. The other boy ran to us, weeping hysterically: 'I met him at the gate and we started to talk. I never saw him before.' A crowd gathered and we followed the ambulance across Kingsbridge to Steven's Hospital. Soon the mother of the boy was helped down half fainting from an outside car. We remained at a safe distance from the crowd for, even in those tragic moments, we did not forget our fear of Protestant institutions, and the legend associated with that hospital was of a peculiar kind. The wealthy Madam Steven had been punished by Heaven for some grave offence and had given birth to a child with a pig's head. She had repented and left a sum of money for a hospital to be founded.

Long before I knew in the dark the click of the magic lantern slide, the mingling odours of oil, heated tin and paint, I saw Poole's myriorama at the Rotunda. Memory still holds a few seconds of glory: world-scenes, gigantic and luminous, moving past. When we were all busy with our sums and exercises in Second or Third Grammar, the bioscope came to that Round Room, which had been a fashionable assembly place in the eighteenth century. Twice a year the Living Pictures were there and, on my way to them, I always stopped at the fountain near the corner to take a gulp of water from the chained iron cup, while the dray horses drew up their steady, yet fussy gallons from the trough half-way around it. In the darkness we watched the future age of speed in which all was quickened – men, women, darting down streets, through doorways, up and down steps, quicker than we could, wheels revolving, the globe itself turning. Some of the fantastic tricks of photography in those experimental years appealed no doubt to adults but often offended schoolboys. We had read our Jules Verne and when *A Journey to the Moon* was presented we were annoyed by several impossibilities; for instance, an express train hurtling through space at an absurd angle and then disappearing into the cracked smile of a pantomime moon. Unfortunately my own delight at the Rotunda was complicated by much misery for I was only allowed fourpence by my parents, so I had to stand or squat in one of the arches around the hall among the urchins from Dorset Street, Wellington Street and Little Britain Street. Whenever the lights went up, I crouched in my corner lest I should be seen by my school companions, the sons of lawyers, doctors and merchants, reclining at their ease in the seats of the pit.

When I was thirteen, James Joyce brought much pleasure to Dublin schoolboys for he established the first permanent cinema in Mary Street. The Volta was opened in 1909 and, needless to say, I was there the first week – on Christmas Eve. The programme was typically Joycean and literary experts tell us that the main film was 'The Tragic Story of Beatrice Cenci'. The theme of incest was beyond my comprehension and, in any case, my attention was distracted for 'Uncle' Harry, a friend of the family who took me to the performance, had just given me my Christmas box and I clutched it firmly on my lap. It was a real cinematograph costing seven and sixpence which he had bought for me in Lawrence's toy shop in Grafton Street half an hour before. I remember, however, very well the other film. It was called 'The First Paris Orphanage' or *La Pouponnière.* Nowadays it would be called a documentary and would hardly have been passed by our film censors. I was shocked by the sight of so many naked children being bathed or running round in glee, dripping and tumbling about. Those little Adams and Eves, turned up to be dried or potted by expert nurses, brought back to me painful memories of a time when I was really too modest to be sitting in the galvanized bath in our kitchen. I dreaded the sudden visits of Uncle John on such occasions for he would point at me mockingly and dart forward. His bodily movements were startling for he had once been the Champion Handball Player of the World. I leaped from the bath and, trying to hide my little thingummy-bob with my hands, fled under the table.

The age of invention had more and more placards. Our thoughts were mostly in the air. They went up hopefully with the Wright Brothers, Bleriot, Farnham, and, as often as not, came down in disappointment. Even the rooks were taken by surprise when the first display of flying machines took place at Leopardstown for they rose in flocks and stayed in the air, chattering and protesting while we craned our necks or inspected the temporary hangars. The *Aero* and other periodicals became for most of us a new kind of home studies and we puzzled over calculations which were more difficult than those we learned at school. My parents were pleased and decided that later on I would become an engineer. For many months I worked in spare time at the construction of a three-foot scale model of the Wright biplane, hurrying occasionally for materials to the tool shops in Capel Street. I was busy with fret-saw, wooden struts, wire stays, glue, testing the mysteries of camber. My mother bought for me the Japanese silk which was to be varnished with shellac; the two propellers had to be shaped from blocks of ash wood and my father got one of his chisels specially sharpened. Indeed, I shed some of my blood in the cause of science for I sliced the ball of my left thumb with the chisel, was conveyed to hospital for seven stitches and still bear the mark. The day came at last when the model was completed. The rubber motors installed and the propellers whirring. Alas! The machine remained heavier than the air and refused to rise. Robinson Crusoe's experience with his first boat was little consolation to me and, as all my measurements and details seemed correct, I felt deeply the injustice of this failure and have never discovered its moral. To make matters worse, my parents changed their minds for, in exercising my wits during that winter, I had completely neglected my lessons. They decided, therefore, that I must be sent to a boarding school. Clongowes was much too costly and so they chose a less expensive Jesuit College a few miles from the city of Limerick. There I was destined to meet a descendant of the author of '*The Lays of Ancient Rome*', and discovered from him the nature of poetry.

IV

On a sunny September morning, at Kingsbridge, I sat beside my parents in the train, a new boy in a new suit. We were expecting two family friends who were travelling to Limerick and there was no sign of them. Just as the whistle sounded, however, the young married couple almost tumbled into the carriage. Scarcely had Elsie sat down when she began breathlessly to blame her husband for causing the delay and nothing could stop her. In vain Charles tried to explain that he had been struggling with a stud for he was wearing a choker like my father. In vain my mother tried to change the conversation but, as the train gathered speed and whirled past Lucan, that pretty young woman was still agitated. Charles was tall, curly-headed and had a small moustache which I had always admired. Suddenly he burst into tears, jumped up and disappeared, banging the communication door after him. I was so astonished at seeing a grown-up man crying that I have forgotten the rest of that journey. But the experience kept back my own tears for the rest of the day. At two o'clock, we were having our 'dinner' with some other friends in a house in a Georgian Street, which might have been in Dublin. A few hours later we set out to see the sights. We hurried through slums to stare at King John's Castle but it started to drizzle as we came to the bridge across the Shannon to inspect the famous Treaty Stone. There the worst happened. Patrick Sarsfield, Earl of Lucan and all his horsemen could scarcely have galloped faster from the Williamite gunpowder dump which they had blown up than I did as I made towards the nearest lane-way, hastily undoing the back buttons of my breeches. I must explain that my mother believed firmly, in her Victorian way, in the necessity of physical as well as spiritual purgation. Every Saturday morning, my sisters and I were given a cup of senna tea sweetened with milk and sugar. My attempts to drink the horrible mixture failed completely and so, instead, on Saturday night, I was given an egg-cupful of cascara sagrada. At first I was unable to take it without help, so my father held my head back while my mother poured the contents of the egg-cup down my throat. My stomach rejected most of it but, like my compulsory spiritual doses, some of it remained inside me. Quite illogically, my mother, in her anxiety for my bowels during the long school term, had given me, on the night before, a pill of immense purgative power and, in the excitement of the journey, I had forgotten all about it till that moment. The rain blurred along the deserted quays as I crept down river steps, chilled and exposed, and crawled back again, still unrelieved. My mother was contrite and my father waited anxiously on guard, as I hid behind garden gates or explored side walks, clutching the last crumpled pages of the *Irish Independent.* After hours of misery and gripe, I was brought, triumphant over adversity and inwardly cleansed, to the college.

Curiously enough, that pill was symbolic because for many years my thoughts of the place were so filthy that I could not peer through the cloacal darkness. The main water closets were outside in what was known as the Square and for boys from Dublin or other cities every visit to them meant a feat of acrobatism. Most of the boarders, however, came from the wilds of Kerry or Clare and evidently had never been house-trained. No doubt they had been accustomed to void themselves behind ditch, stable or the ruins of the nearest ancient tower. The concrete floors, the seat-rims, the pipes were thick with the ordure of past terms and the newest slotter of the week. Until the winter rains came, it was quite impossible to escape the stench for, on the warm September days, the west wind blew it across the playing fields.

The Jesuit poet, Gerard Manley Hopkins, died of typhoid, a victim, it is said, of the defective drains at St. Patrick's House, Dublin. We were more fortunate than the frail English convert. No doubt the holy fathers meant well, but all of them were middle-aged and apparently not very practical. In my own case, I suffered as much from the food as from the constant sight of its waste products. Our breakfast consisted of bread and butter, tea. Our main meal had been planned by those who had long since passed away and was full of good intentions: a joint, potatoes, vegetables, pudding. Unfortunately, contractors, left to themselves, can be dishonest, and kitcheners indifferent or careless. So the joint appeared always old, grizzly, blue-veined, over-done; the store potatoes half black or soapy; the cabbage or turnips watery; the pudding tasteless, except on Fridays, when we had jam tart which was delicious, despite the stiffness of the pastry. Money is sacred in this land and there was deplorable discrimination in our refectory. Boys, whose parents could afford to pay extra, sat at a special table eating a speckled egg at breakfast, and at eleven o'clock, we could see them hurrying in for a glass of milk. For our evening meal we had tea, bread and butter. All the boarders must have written home as repeatedly as I did because our lockers were supplied with slabs of brown and yellow cake and we had an unusual supply of money to expend at the tuck-shop. Sometimes after the Mass at seven-thirty of a winter's morning, a few city boys, including myself, would steal around a corner of the corridor to the forbidden quarter while the priests from the various oratories were divesting themselves. There, with home longings, we enjoyed the smell of frying rashers and eggs.

Whenever a new boy arrived after term had started, another boy was given a free day in order to show him around the college and the grounds. This was an excellent custom for it meant an immediate friend and perhaps in the future a useful champion. Jack MacCurtain was gay, debonair, and a few minutes after we met he was hurrying with me down the corridors, past the murmurs of the class-rooms, to show me the printed set of rules on a notice board. Gleefully he pointed out the last and most important rule, which sternly forbade us all to keep our hands in our trouser pockets. From that day Jack was my champion and helped me in many small difficulties. However, there was little bullying and the senior boys, though some were fearsome to look at, left us in peace. Jack could not protect me, however, from my own folly and, though it is dangerous to play with tigers, I could not resist teasing one. The Tiger, as he was nicknamed, was about my own age, sturdy, low-sized, red-headed and respected for his ferocious temper. Obviously I had gone too far one day and the other boys quickly formed a ring around us during recreation. A prefect passed by and, seeing that all was fair, disappeared around the corner of the quadrangle. I had been trained in boxing by my father, had darted daily round an old punch ball at home and later, at college, Sergeant Wright of the British Army had given us more formidable instruction. I preferred, however, the sharp rap of fisticuffs to the smothering nose-squashing blow of boxing gloves. My foot-work was good – but would I be able to dodge the powerful blows of my opponent? As soon as the signal was given, the Tiger, flouting all rules, charged at me furiously, head down. I stepped aside and gave him a quick upper cut as he passed. He looked surprised, retreated back to his corner and, with raised fists and lowered head, charged again. I stepped aside and gave him another upper cut. Six times he charged in the same way and each time I had to repeat the same simple tactics for my own safety until at last the other boys led the poor little creature away, bloodied and confounded. I proved that I was not a milksop and a few days later, when my parents obtained permission for me to quit the rugby field and practise the violin instead, the other boys accepted my lack of interest in outdoor sports.

My interest in music was becoming less but it gave me a special advantage. Once a week, on the half holiday, all of us were permitted, in small groups, to visit Limerick. I had an extra free afternoon of my own and went there for a music lesson to Mr. Vincent. He was tall, pale, languid, and I felt there was some mystery about him because of the collection of extraordinary statuettes in his room. On mantelpiece, shelves and side tables were rows of these statuettes, all of naked or half-naked women and men in different poses, so startlingly white in the sunlight that there were times when I could scarcely see my minims on the music stand. Mr. Vincent never referred to these indecent objects and since then I have often wondered about him. Had he found a refuge in pagan art from the oppressiveness of provincial life? Even at that time the wicked English Sunday newspapers were burned occasionally in the streets of Limerick, and these acts of piety were praised in our national press. When Sousa and his Yankee Band came to the city for a single performance, I was present with my music master. The theatre shook with the mighty blowings, bangs and thumpings, but I was delighted with the Big Noise and all its boastfulness without realizing that I was listening for the first time to the music of a coming Great Power.

Most of the Jesuit masters in that school are lost for me in shadows, even their nicknames gone. Only a few oddities and moments are left: Belly Tomkins, our kindly Rector, showing us simple conjuring tricks in his study, a pauper skull on his desk; Scaldy, old, remote, bored with teaching us Latin, his face suddenly filled with a warm light as he slowly spoke for us a few lines of Homer so that we might hear in the Greek words the twang of bow and the hiss of arrow; portly Father O'Mahony, our Prefect of Studies, black pores around his tormented nose, fumbling at the old cotton handkerchief which stuck out of his pocket, filthy with brown stains, a snuff addict, whose pinches of vice, blowings and wipings filled us with wonder; Father O'Leary, small, dark, alert, hurrying in his soutane across the quadrangle to find out if the earth had shaken during the night. We knew that Father O'Leary was a great scientist and, therefore, he was in charge of the seismograph of which we were all so proud. This instrument was in a small building to itself and I was disappointed when I was brought to see it, having in the course of my earlier aeronautical studies pored over the diagrams of the internal combustion engine. The suspended weight was hidden and all that could be seen was what appeared to be a barograph.

Nevertheless earth tremors were very real to us for had we not in our school a master who had escaped from the San Francisco earthquake? Thomas Babington Macaulay Fell may have been a failure but he triumphs over those shadowy figures in the past. Secondary education is a religious monopoly but, as a concession to public opinion every college has at least one lay teacher. Mr. Fell, who taught us English and elocution, was an Englishman, an ex-actor and a convert. He claimed to be a direct descendant of the poet-historian and we were as proud of his claim as he was. We all knew that Lord Macaulay had declared that the Catholic Church would still be prevailing against its foes when London Bridge had fallen down: and here, before us, as visible proof, was one of his descendants, converted from error. He was tall, aquiline, his greying hair heavily oiled and brushed back from his forehead and he was always dressed in blue serge. One day, as he was declaiming for us a long passage towards the end of Longfellow's *Hiawatha*, which describes how the hero parts from his people, launches his birch canoe and sets out across the water for the last time, the class-room and all the boys in it disappeared and I saw the pinewoods, the creeks and the glitter of unknown waters. With the last words the extraordinary vision disappeared and Mr. Fell was back again on the rostrum. This was my first experience of the evocative power of verbal rhythm and it brought back my earlier experiences of Nature. I had almost forgotten them because the Clare Mountains which we could see across the Shannon from the upper windows in the wintry light were bare and grim.

Mr. Fell produced the college plays and the first which I saw was very moving and edifying. The scenes took place in contemporary France, where the world was witnessing the most violent and vicious campaign against religion that history had yet seen. The whole power and resources of the wicked were organised against religion and there were traitors everywhere. But the French President was punished for his persecutory and atheistic zeal. His son, a young Jesuit priest, faced a riotous mob and was mortally wounded. He died, clasped by his weeping, repentant father.

One evening, Mr. Fell took a few of us to his room on the first landing to make us up, for we were taking part in a concert sketch. The room, which had a gothic doorway, was no larger than a monastic cell and the six of us huddled into it as best we could, delighted by his confusion of treasures: photos, pictures, costumes, grease paints, cream pots. Rapidly the great man made us up and then, sitting down on the truckle bed, began to talk with such vehemence and in such detail that we were completely puzzled. He had been treated unjustly and with ingratitude despite his hard work and conscientiousness. He might be only an Englishman, but he was not ashamed of it, though he was treated with that contempt and ingratitude. He had been producing the college plays, for many years and all of us knew that his production of them was excellent, but there were certain priests who were enemies of his and had been spreading lies about him. It was a perfect disgrace and now what did we think had happened? He was no longer allowed to produce plays for the apostolics and they had set up a rival group, but he would show them that our house productions were better. As the old actor was almost in tears when we left him, we were very much embarrassed.

Despite our mystification, we shared with all the other lay boys the resentment of Mr. Fell against the apostolics, for we were not permitted to meet this superior species. Although the seminary was attached to the college, we never saw or heard its students except at a distance when they were playing football. They were guarded completely from contact with us, so that we could not help feeling that we were inferiors. This feeling was increased by the fact that the Fathers constantly gave us examples of the wickedness of the outer world, from which the apostolics had to be protected. During the summer before my first term, one of the apostolics, because of his tender years, had to be kept in the college during the holidays for there was a British military camp near his home. We often thought of that boy of thirteen with the whole seminary to himself, its silent corridors, its empty sports fields.

Tuberculosis has been our national disease and the fact that it was so prevalent among the young of the middle class could be attributed not only to late dances but to malnutrition in clerical schools and institutions. During my second term at Mungret, my health rapidly declined owing to a lack of proper nourishment. I was taken away hastily by my parents, given plenty of eggs, milk, butter and soon recovered.

Before I left, however, I had a slight experience of the moral dangers in institutions which are entirely male. The senior students were given special privileges; they had a recreation room of their own and were even allowed to smoke an occasional cigarette. One of these students suddenly took an interest in me and I was much pleased by his friendship and generosity. For three weeks he plied me with sweets, slipping them into my hand as he passed by or pushing them into my pocket. I was a little puzzled but I respected the secrecy of it all and ate them greedily whenever I was by myself. Evidently the seduction had been carefully planned for one evening, when I was in the study- room, a message came that I was wanted and I was given permission to leave. Waiting outside in the corridor was my new friend and he led me to the wash-room. There, awkward and ill-at-ease, he muttered a mysterious sentence to me. I have never forgotten it for it might have been a literal translation from our Irish phrase book, *tabhair dham spúnóg*. I was frightened and hurried away but he did not follow me. When I returned to the Study, I noticed that many of the boys glanced at me cautiously from their lesson books and I felt that they knew what that knock at the door had meant. The priest in charge was obviously unaware of their significant curiosity.

The Jesuit Fathers accepted the Victorian belief that the problems of puberty could be solved by the playing of British games, such as cricket and rugby. Some weeks after my own experience, there was a great sensation in the school when Father O'Mahony discovered the respective captains of the two Junior rugby teams in bed together. They were offered the alternative of immediate expulsion or flogging. No doubt the mildness of this punishment was due to the necessity of keeping the scandal from spreading beyond the college.

There is no doubt that a country in which an ever-increasing number of celibate orders continually exert influence must suffer from a hidden uneasiness. No theologian nowadays believes with Aquinas in succubation; no vow of chastity can prevent man or youth experiencing natural pleasure in what a merry hedge-schoolmaster of the Penal Age used to call *somnium humidissimum*. Our hidden war against natural instinct was intensified as soon as we had gained our freedom and the British troopships sailed from our southern harbours. While Mr. de Valera's republican army and the new regiments of Mr. Cosgrave's Provisional Government were jeering one another in the streets of Dublin and the Civil War was imminent, the suppressors of vice were already active. Despatch riders patrolled the city lane-ways at night time in search of skirt-lifters. Led by a friar, devoted bands closed down the brothel district by means which were not strictly legal but had the secret approval of the new Government. In a few years there were several serious outbreaks of what used to be called unnatural vice. Latrines were razed and the unfortunate touchers of Dublin were rounded up. In some cases ferocious sentences of five to seven years in prison were given by our new judges.

Fourteen

I

I TURNED seaward from the road at Dollymount and, as I wheeled my bicycle on to the thin wooden bridge, I could only hear the sound of my own steps on the planks and the minute whirr of the ball bearings. I looked northward towards Howth and then, as I clambered down the boulders of the breakwater, I could see, through the timeless air, the seventh city of Christendom. Disconsolate, I raised my eyes towards the slow drifting clouds, dappled and Wicklow-borne. Far away, across the estuary, were the mountain ranges and most of my school companions were among them, for this was the day of the annual picnic. In another hour they would be at the Glen o' the Downs or, perhaps, in the Devil's Glen, eating their luncheon, fearlessly hurrying from the sunlight into the woods. This was the first year in which I had not gained the requisite numbers of weekly marks which would entitle me to go, and so I was one of three or four in my class who had been excluded. My mother had made up some sandwiches for me but my attempt to have a picnic on my own was a failure. I was aware of the loneliness of sea and sky on that week-day and brooded over my disgrace.

After I had left the boarding school, I had been sent back to Belvedere and some unaccountable change happened to me. Every thing went wrong. I neglected my lessons, I was careless and indifferent: The more I struggled and blundered, the more some contrary presence seemed to possess my mind. That confusion and mental dimness in which I seemed lost are hard to recall but I have no doubt this is the state in which so many young delinquents, as they are called today, find themselves. Aggrieved, deeply hurt, they feel that they have been betrayed and do not know what has happened to them.

Despite the confusion and occultation of that year, a few impressions come back to me. Ostensibly the Devereux twins were our ringleaders in pranks and caused much amusement in class by their quick changing of place when the master's back was turned for they were almost identical both in appearance and voice. Soon, however, our entire class was troubled by the problems of puberty and that common secret could no longer be concealed. Andrews took charge – a plump little fellow, whose eyes went baw-wise whenever he took off his glasses to wipe them. The glee he took in priapic knowledge was extraordinary. He was delighted by his own ducts and was constantly asking us if we had ever been tumefied. On one occasion he showed us some indecent snaps of his sisters, asquat, but these snaps were badly developed and too blurred to be tell-tale. I was so horrified by his wickedness that I asked 'Nigger' Johnson one day to explain to me the facts of life. His voice was so deep that even his whisper was a rumble. Gravely and as patiently as a sex instructor today in English schools, he explained to me and illustrated the facts with rapid drawings on a page of his copy-book. My mind, however, lacked due preparation and for several years afterwards refused absolutely to accept the uro-genital design, regarding it as a proposition of the Devil. I was convinced that my nipples must have a purpose and I confirmed this by consulting our Douai Bible. In the Songs of Solomon, I found the words: 'He lay betwixt my breasts', and they gave me a delicate, dreamy feeling: I was certain, therefore, that conception took place not in a gross way but ethereally by the gentle touch of the male and female paps.

The secret furor of our class was not allayed by the calm, constant presence of our Prefect of Studies. Father Boyle moved quickly, quietly as a spirit and his lips moved almost imperceptibly in prayer. The Jesuit apostle of Peru, Father Diego Martinez, repeated over 4,000 aspirations daily. Father Boyle endeavoured to reach a daily total of 25,000 aspirations and sometimes achieved 10,000 before lunch. Indeed, no prayer-wheel could have been faster. In his warfare against the evils of the flesh, he was unable to undertake long fasts or reduce his diet owing to the conditions of community life. When he tried to take a smaller helping of beef or mutton, refused the apple tart or pudding, anxious inquiries were made about his loss of appetite. Flagellation can be overheard and so Father Boyle devised silent methods of subduing nature. Being under a vow of obedience, he had to obtain permission from his spiritual superior for his acts of austerity. Most of his experiments in pain were not, however, practical: he tried to cut the Holy Name of Jesus on his chest with a razor blade but suffered too much loss of blood, and the application of a heated iron caused ugly dangerous sores. His last attempt was almost fatal. He was giving a retreat in a convent near Greystones and one evening, passing a lonely wood, saw a bed of nettles. Hastily stripping, he jumped into the bed, rolled among the nettles and was severely poisoned.

Already death was moving towards that class in Belvedere. A few years later, on the outbreak of the war between England, France and Germany, our Prefect of Studies became a military chaplain and, among the thousands in the Irish Division was killed at the Battle of Ypres. Many of my class-mates, including one of the Devereux twins, and my favourite companion, Ollie, died fighting for King and Country.

II

In these days when ancient gutturals go against the gorge, and all aspiration is compulsory, it is pleasant to think of a time when the Irish language had a slightly illegal aspect. There must have been faint stirrings of national recovery in the years before the Rising. For, one sunny morning, the rector of our highly respectable school announced that there would be an Irish class for those who wished to take that subject. Shamefacedly, a few of us put up our hands, impelled by some vague memories of Brian Boru and the Dalcassians, little suspecting the social torments which we were to endure.

The new lay master arrived, and when he stumped into the class-room we realized that he had a wooden leg. In addition, he had a strange stare, but we never could find out whether his left eye was really made of glass. We endured the scorn of our more respectable school companions until in a few months the teacher disappeared. We awaited with some anxiety the coming of the next Irish master. One of his hands was gloved and, to our consternation, we saw that he had an artificial arm. By this time we had all concluded that there was something very queer about the Irish language. Moreover, the new master made strange clucking noises which had nothing to do with Gaelic eclipsis, and at times pinched us behind the blackboard. But his generosity and good humour endeared him to us so that we almost forgave him his physical blemishes. He, too, disappeared with disconcerting haste. Our last Irish master at school was unblemished. But at a time when serge alone was respectable, he wore thick tweeds, a country cap, and leggings. He, too, disappeared – to South America.

Schoolboys at that time were interested in the new mystery of aeroplane construction, the mathematical problems of helices and air resistance, and so we felt that the complexity of Irish grammar was at variance with the simplicity of the subject matter. We were always opening and closing the door. The cup was for ever on the board. We inquired daily for the little white cat. The pig, the hen, the cow and the ass were the unceasing topics of our crude stammers. Yet, as a city youngster, I found excitement and strangeness in this mental farm life. One pleasure was denied us in those days of British rule. We could not jingle a halfpenny with a pig on it against a penny with a hen and three chicks. On our birthday we could not possess a silver horse or leaping salmon on a florin.

I had, a premonitory glimpse of the pagan Gaelic era, for on our course was *Eisirt*, an early story, from which Dean Swift is said to have borrowed the idea of Lilliput. Even in our modernized version, the poetic parts kept their incantatory power and I was inspired by lines such as these, which I give from Standish Hayes O'Grady's translation in *Silva Gaedelica*:

> Burn not the precious apple-tree of spreading and low-sweeping bough; tree ever decked in bloom of white, against whose fair head all men put forth the hand. The surly blackthorn is a wanderer, and a wood that the artificer burns not: throughout its body, though it be scanty, birds in their flocks warble. The noble willow burn not, a tree sacred to poems: with his bloom bees are a-sucking, all love the little cage. The graceful tree with the berries, the wizard's tree, the rowan, burn: but spare the limber tree: burn not the slender hazel.

As an undergraduate I escaped at one step from the snobbery of school life and discovered the Love Songs of Connaught, those poems and translations which had started our Literary Revival.

Their poet-translator was on the rostrum, and, though I could not always follow the swift rush of Dr. Hyde's western Irish, I knew from his gestures that he was speaking a living language. When the future President of Eire enacted *Casadh an tSugain* for us, he took the parts of all the characters, jumping up and down from the rostrum in his excitement, and, as he unwound an imaginary straw rope at the end of the play, found himself outside the lecture room.

On the morning of our first term, he spoke of the aims and ideals of the language revival: we were all equal, all united in the Gaelic movement. There was no vulgar competition, no showing-off, no twopence-halfpenny looking down on twopence. Those plain words changed me in a few seconds. The hands of our lost despised centuries were laid on me.

To meet Dr. Sigerson, the last of the great pioneers, was to become aware of a distant Victorian period when our literary traditions were saved from extinction by a few idealists. From him I learned about the subtle art of our formal poetry. Then, to complete so much good fortune, there was Stephen MacKenna – moody, eloquent, a man consumed by some inner flame. He would, turn from Rabelais to roll out some passionate protest of Ua Bruadair, forget Plotinus to denounce those who belittled the elegance of Carolan and failed to appreciate his rhythmic improvisations

Padraic O'Conairé was always in disgrace, though the 'unco' guid' have now raised a statue to him in Galway. His past in London was mysterious. Had he really tramped across Russia to argue with Tolstoi? Had he been truly tutor to the King of Spain's daughter? As he tapped his way down Grafton Street, with ragged coat and battered hat, many a wearer of the fáinne slipped around the corner. He was tolerant of my mistakes in Irish grammar, and taught me to drink like a man. One morning at five o'clock we left Mabbot Street, made our way to the City Market, drank stout with the dealers there and then wandered through Wicklow for a week.

By little Connaught
When sails were filling
And shadow danced like a balladman,
What should I hear
As I leaned on the counter
But the ferrule of O'Conairé

Hitting the road
To Tirnanogue!
And, O Padraic you did not know me,
Though we, for week
In Baltinglass,
Were drinking with the Wicklow men.

But all this happened in the days when the language was not bought or sold, and nobody thought of what Yeats has called 'the heavier purse'.

III

I was discovering very slowly my nationality and, no doubt, the scorn with which our Irish class in school had been regarded was an incitement. I was much troubled, however, when, the 1914 war broke out and so many of my former school companions hastened to join up.

As an undergraduate at University College, I, too, had just reached military age. There was a much-abused minority, but Dublin rallied to the colours. Our Home Rule leaders held enthusiastic recruiting meetings at College Green, and I found it hard to resist the moving words of Stephen Gwynn, whose text book, *The Masters of English Literature*, was on our course. Tall, handsome in his officer's uniform, he seemed to be calling to me in the crowd, but I was timid and so perplexed by the mystery of my own existence that I did not wish to deprive anyone else of his. So I sneaked past the posters which implored us all to fight for Catholic Belgium, and avoided Grafton Street, where girls waited with white feathers to decorate shirkers like myself. I needed some excuse, however, and, as chance would have it, a relative from England gave me some pamphlets published by the Independent Labour Party, and in them I read Roger Casement's reports on the torture and mutilation of the natives of the Congo by the Belgians. Nevertheless, in all those years of the war, it was impossible to forget the distant horror.

An immediate problem still remained unsolved and it was in my own home. One of our recent family friends was a jolly English military man, who was stationed at the nearby barracks. Several evenings a week he came to visit us and keep the decanter busy. I have always suffered from our national defect of moral cowardice and particularly so at that age. During those first weeks of the war, I crept into our house, hoping that Captain Rumbold would soon be sent off with his regiment. One evening, however, he caught me in the passage at the side-door. Pointing an accusing finger at me, like Lord Kitchener in the recruiting poster, he exclaimed:

'You've ben 'iding from me and I know the reason why.' Then his brown eyes twinkled and he laughed. He became grave again and said, 'Keep out of it, my lad.' Merry again, he explained that he was unfit for military service owing to fallen arches and had just been given a clerical post at a higher salary in the War Office. I was considerably surprised for I had not as yet read *Arms and the Man.*

IV

Mr. Dempsey, our English master, seemed to me a very aristocratic figure and I was much in awe of him. He lived on the south side of the city, spoke well, and dressed nattily. As he was the only permanent lay teacher employed in our school, his light grey suit, his spotless linen, seemed all the more elegant in contrast to the black soutanes of our other instructors. He kept his hands spread on each side of his paunch and continually sucked peppermints and this puzzled me. I was equally puzzled by his expression which seemed sardonic, but it might have been only due to indigestion and the weariness of years.

The British educational system in our country at that time must have been odd: yet I owe much to it. The English prose text on our Senior Intermediate Course was *Dreamthorpe*, a collection of essays, by a Scottish poet, who has been ridiculed by the critics of the Victorian age. Those essays of Alexander Smith captivated me and before I knew what had happened to me, I was no longer, at the bottom of the class but at the top, and Mr. Dempsey was reading out passages from my weekly composition with highly flattering remarks. Young minds are complicated and, despite myself, I could not really like him. During my period of mental obscurity, he had ignored me completely and my sudden emergence into a condition of lucidity was as inexplicable to me as my year of sullenness and disgrace. Nevertheless, his old-fashioned method of teaching was certainly effective. The verse text which the Commissioners had chosen for Irish schools was by the Latin Secretary to Cromwell, whose name is still a curse here. Week by week, passage by passage, we committed the First Book of *Paradise Lost* to memory and at the end of the year most of us, if necessary, could recite the whole without hesitation, and equally by rote we knew the copious notes and explanatory references. Gradually the Vision of the great Puritan poet eliminated from my mind the last fears of the hell of Alighieri, in which, cut up, boiled, roasted, our bits had shrieked through the years of infancy and boyhood. Imaginatively I ventured into the visible darkness, moved by the lakes of burning marl, peered into pandemonium and admired those majestic fallen angels, who, despite continual pain, spoke so proudly and with such courage. Their secondary names brought me glimpses of other mythologies – Mulciber, Dagon, Baalim, Ashtaroth, Thammuz. The speeches of revolt stirred my mind so that I forgot the grovelling and insincerity of our medieval training. The next world had become a mental refuge. So much did I feel the power of Milton's imaginative vision that, when years later, a poet led the High Church Party attack on him, I could not have been more indignant if I had been purely English, nor have felt more afflicted by it.

Although I had been conditioned from a tender age, I can remember little of the gradual process of indoctrination. There are, however, certain names and words which I cannot hear without, an involuntary shudder: for instance, Henry VIII, Darwin, evolution. Socialism, also, is a word which almost makes me murmur a protective aspiration despite my interest in Irish reform. There must have been Labour unrest in the Dublin slums when I was at school for our saintly Prefect of Studies, Father Boyle, left us to hold retreats for workmen. These were held in honour of the Workman of Nazareth, hardly an apt appelation. Needless to say, Father Boyle was soon collecting funds for the building of a suitable Retreat House. By this time my conditioning must have been almost complete as one instance will show. In the fields behind the terrace on the North Circular Road, on which we lived, I played sometimes with four or five Protestant lads. They had a curious habit of searching the grass, picking and eating what they called goats' currants. They assured me that these vegetable droppings were very sweet and pleasant to the taste. I refused to be tempted and came to the conclusion that these little cricketers belonged to a different species. Often, when I am talking to Protestants, I catch myself wondering whether they, too, were coprophagists in their early years.

During our last year of religious instruction in school, we were given a course of apologetics so that, steeled within the commandery of Loyola, we would be on our guard against the dangers of the world. Our text book was a squat volume, with buff-coloured paper covers, and of enormous value for its low price. It was called *The Question Box* and consisted of queries made by anxious searchers for the truth, followed by the requisite answers. Having been brought up by my parents to believe that proselytism was a purely Protestant activity, I was surprised – but probably in those days of British rule our poaching in other religious stew-ponds was nocturnal. I was even more surprised when I realized for the first time that what I had supposed to be plain facts, were beliefs which had to be defended by argument. Although I had no words for my thoughts, I realized dimly that we, too, could exercise private judgment on condition that we agreed with the arguments given to us. The first question in the book was about the existence of God, and the Jesuit compilers, in order to reassure their querists, used the argument from design by a well-known Protestant theologian. Unfortunately Paley's example of the watch made me suspicious, for I remembered that day in class when a young priest had shown us his gold hunter and told us humbly that it did not really belong to him. To add to my spiritual troubles, I had a small silver hunter of my own inlaid with blue numerals, which my father, in his generosity, had given me for a birthday present. It had, however, brought me more misery than pleasure for, despite the jewels in it, the works were imperfect and the tick often stopped. Moreover, when other boys admired it, asked how much it cost and in what shop it had been bought, I was ashamed to tell them that it was secondhand and my replies had to be evasive. Soon I became much more interested in the questions in the book than in the answers, being secretly thrilled by the audacity of them. No subject was too sacred to be accepted without clear proofs: the Incarnation, the Virgin Birth, Transubstantiation, the Resurrection of the Body – all were doubted by these extraordinuy people. Before I came to the last page, I suspect that I had become, without knowing it, an Arian.

William Sharp, better known as Fiona McLeod, has told us that in his early years he experienced 'a wonderful momentary dazzle in the brain'. Without guessing anything about symbolism, I delighted in the first line and a half of *Paradise Lost*, fervently rejecting the implied consequences. I watched frequently the Tree of Knowledge and – whether my eyes were closed or wide open – its bark and all its boughs were glittering.

Index

Austin Clarke was born in Dublin's Manor Street in May, 1896. He was educated at Belvedere College and University College, Dublin. His first publication was a long poem *The Vengeance of Fionn* which appeared in 1917 to critical acclaim and went into a second edition. From then until his death in 1974 Clarke published some twenty volumes of poems, over half of them published under the Bridge Press imprint in limited editions of about two hundred copies, three novels *The Bright Temptation* (1932), *The Singing Men at Cashel* (1936) and *The Sun Dances at Easter* (1952), all of which were banned by the Irish Censorship Board, two volumes of reminiscences *Twice Round the Black Church* (1962) and *A Penny in the Clouds* (1968) and over a dozen verse plays.

In 1932 Clarke was elected a founder member of the Irish Academy of Letters, became its president in 1952 and received its major literary award, the Gregory Medal, in 1968. He spent some seventeen years in England where he reviewed books in various papers such as the *Daily News and Leader, The News Chronicle* and *The Spectator*. Returning to Dublin in 1937 he reviewed books for *The Irish Times* (1940-1962 and 1968-1973) and *The Irish Press* (1962-1968) and had a weekly poetry programme on the national radio station Radio Eireann for about thirty years.